HEART AND SOUL
CUISINE
FROM THE ESTATES OF SUNNYBROOK

Canadian Cataloguing in Publication Data

Adjey, David, 1964-
    Heart and soul cuisine from the estates of Sunnybrook

Includes index.
ISBN 0-9681344-1-6

1. Low-fat diet – Recipes. 2. Salt-free diet – Recipes.
I. Holley, Janice, 1962- II. Sunnybrook Health Science Centre. III. Title.

RC684.D5A34 1997   641-5'638   C97-931143-8

Photography: Curtis Trent
Cover and interior design: Gillian Tsintziras, The Brookview Group Inc.
Editor: Cynthia David

Published by:
The Estates of Sunnybrook and the Heart and Circulation Program
Sunnybrook Health Science Centre, University of Toronto
Toronto, Ontario, Canada

2nd Printing
Printed and bound in Canada by University of Toronto Press Inc.
Toronto, Ontario

Front cover: Lobster, Lobster, Lobster! (p. 124)

To my children, Jamie Lee and Ryan
D.A.

To my parents and family
J.H.

Contents

Acknowledgements

The Estates of Sunnybrook are two of the most splendid mansions in Ontario, spread over 52 acres of stately gardens and walkways on the campus of Sunnybrook Health Science Centre.

The combination of a sophisticated atmosphere, personalized service and close proximity to downtown Toronto make McLean House and Vaughan Estate the ideal location for private, professional conferences or exclusive social events. The beauty and charm of these 67-year-old homes are unparalleled.

Revenues generated by The Estates contribute to medical research at Sunnybrook.

The Sunnybrook Health Science Centre, established in 1948, was initially built to serve the medical needs of World War II veterans. The present multi-faceted facility delivers more intensive and state-of-the-art health care services.

The centre's Heart and Circulation Program is on the cutting edge of providing excellence in cardiovascular services at the local, provincial and national levels. As knowledge about heart disease increases, it is becoming more widely understood as a major health issue for the entire population.

Sunnybrook's Heart and Circulation Program has built a team of clinicians, scientists and researchers, all specialists in heart and circulatory diseases. Harnessing their expertise will have a great impact on a health problem that has major significance in our lives.

This book is made possible through the generous contributions of The Estates of Sunnybrook and the Heart and Circulation Program of Sunnybrook Health Science Centre, University of Toronto.

All proceeds from the sale of this cookbook go directly toward supporting the ongoing financial needs of these programs at Sunnybrook Health Science Centre.

Acknowledgements by Janice

To E. Jane deLacy, RN, M.H.Sc., Director of Operations, Clinical Services and Heart and Circulation Program, and to Dr. Brian W. Gilbert, MD, FRCPC, FACC, Vice President, Cardiovascular Services and Head, Division of Cardiology, whose financial support and enthusiasm for this book, from its inception through completion, made its production possible.

To Emily Phillips and Crystal O'Leary, RD, my clinical nutrition partners in the Heart and Circulation program. Thank you for providing exceptional clinical coverage for me during the final weeks of work on this book. Each of you continually demonstrated actions above and beyond the call of duty.

To Rhona Nayman, RD, CNSD, who supported my dream to write a cookbook. Thank you for your encouragement to pursue this project, and for your many devoted hours spent reviewing the manuscript.

To all my clinical nutrition colleagues and the team members in the Heart and Circulation Program at Sunnybrook who motivated and inspired me with their continual support, interest and excitement for the book.

To Lorna Lawrence, M.Sc., RD, my dear friend and mentor for over 11 years, who taught me the importance of striving for excellence in serving others. The professional training I received from Lorna has become an integral part of the way I practise nutrition today.

To Joan McLaughlin, M.H.Sc., RD, a dynamic leader and coach, who opened the door to professional writing for me early in my nutrition career through her innovative project ideas.

Most important of all, I wish to thank my best friend and cherished husband, Lester, whose lavish attention and patience, support and understanding are unwavering in everything that I set out to accomplish. For all of the computer expertise, cheerleading, financial advice and behind-the-scenes planning, I thank you from the bottom of my heart.

Acknowledgements by David

To Kirk Brady, Managing Director of The Estates of Sunnybrook, whose initial enthusiasm was instrumental in getting this project off the ground.

To Joan Fisher, Catering Sales Manager at The Estates of Sunnybrook. Thanks for your warmth, encouragement and for believing in this book.

To Mike Sabo and Mike Owen, my chefs at McLean House and Vaughan Estate. Thanks for keeping everything running smoothly while I tackled this book. To the rest of my kitchen staff, thanks for doing your best every day.

To Andrew Waddington, my trusted apprentice and friend for the past three years. Thank you for your contribution and for being an integral part of this book. I couldn't have finished it without you.

I would like to thank my parents, David and June, for always being there for me and for their encouragement when I needed it most.

Finally, to my wife Laura for her love, understanding and patience over the past 13 years.

General Acknowledgements

In addition to our personal acknowledgements, we would like to express our gratitude to the front-line and hands-on team of experts who worked with us on this enormous project. Their many gifts and talents have produced a book that we can all take pride in. They include:

Curtis Trent, Photographer: For his vision in making our culinary presentations come alive with his photography. Thank you for your energy, time and patience throughout the endless hours of photo shoots.

Gillian Tsintziras, Art Director, The Brookview Group Inc: For co-ordinating the elements of art and design so vividly displayed from cover to cover. Thank you for your guidance and support throughout the entire production process.

Cynthia David, Editor: For keeping our manuscript grounded and consumer-friendly. And we thought we had a clean copy to start with!

Vinay P. Saldanha: For his invaluable assistance.

Reg Hunt and the print production crew, University of Toronto Press Inc.: For their professionalism and enthusiasm.

Bert Knol, Globe Hotelware: For allowing us to borrow the entire contents of his show room for our photographs.

Gail Ryan and Marjorie Agnew, The Main Course: For kindly furnishing us with photography props.

Marshall and Susan Cohen of Eglinton Fine Foods.

Preface

When it comes to healthy eating, myths and misconceptions abound. This cookbook should help clarify that eating can be what we want it to be – appealing, delicious and nutritious.

This is no ordinary cookbook. Our clinical dietitian, Janice Holley, has listened to what our clients and their families need and teamed up with executive chef David Adjey of The Estates of Sunnybrook. Together, they bring you this exciting collection of our own Estate recipes, suited to your heart-seasoned appetite.

Sunnybrook Health Science Centre is a University of Toronto academic teaching hospital as well as a community hospital. The Heart and Circulation Program is one of its priority programs. Primary and secondary prevention of heart disease is an important aspect of our daily interactions with patients, an important part of the teaching program and an important feature of research activities. Thus, the development of a heart-healthy cookbook is an extension of our commitment to you.

One can, at best, prevent and possibly control heart disease with active living, risk factor modification and a healthy diet. We encourage you to adopt our vision through your enjoyment of this cookbook.

Dr. Brian W. Gilbert, MD, FRCPC, FACC
Vice President, Cardiovascular Services
Head, Division of Cardiology

About the Authors

Chefs and dietitians make unlikely kitchenmates. For what would a classically-trained chef do without his cream and butter? And doesn't everyone know that a good measure of salt is one of the secrets of haute cuisine?

Lowering the fat while keeping recipes delicious was the task facing executive chef David Adjey and registered dietitian Janice Holley when they began working on this book more than a year ago, in response to the increasing demand for heart-healthy recipes from their clients. They have truly given their heart and soul to the creation of this work for you.

David describes the experience as "eye-opening". He recalls taking the recipes he loves best and stripping away the fat and salt. He then had to rebuild each dish, filling in the gaps with layers of new flavours. Today, the tools of his trade include red hot chili oil and savoury spice mixes, ethnic ingredients like tandoori paste, puréed fresh herbs and vegetables, even home-made ketchup. These ingredients have one goal – to make each dish so pleasurable, and so full of bold flavours, that you won't miss the fat.

Toronto-born David, who began cooking by his mother's side at the age of five, says he always wanted to be a chef. Even before finishing high school, he had logged many hours as an apprentice. It took several more years of hard work to fulfil one of his greatest ambitions, to attend the prestigious Culinary Institute of America in Hyde Park, New York. Working in New York City under Richard Krause at Melrose inspired him further. Back in Toronto, he worked for some of our most innovative chefs, including Mark McEwan and Greg Couillard. The Left Bank restaurant offered him his first Chef de Cuisine position.

A Certified Chef de Cuisine with the American Culinary Federation and a member of the Canadian Federation of Chefs de Cuisine and the International Association of Culinary Professionals, David is actively pursuing his life-long goal of becoming a Certified Master Chef.

Teaching heart-healthy nutrition to clients, colleagues and the general public is a challenge Janice Holley approaches with great energy and enthusiasm. After graduating in 1985 from the University of Manitoba with a Bachelor's degree in Food and Nutrition, Janice completed a one-year clinical nutrition internship at Sunnybrook to become a Registered Dietitian. Having practised cardiology nutrition for over 11 years, the past eight as a clinical dietitian in the hospital's Heart and Circulation Program, she makes it a priority to keep abreast of research trends and popular literature in order to answer the many questions that confront her daily.

A recognized expert in assisting clients in setting realistic goals for behaviour change, Janice finds her work extremely rewarding. "Most people know everything about how to diet, yet few know how to stop dieting," she says. "The publication of this cookbook is the culmination of my goal to produce a tool that will help people overcome their obsession with dieting."

Janice is a member of the College of Dietitians of Ontario, Dietitians of Canada, Consulting Dietitians of Ontario, Organization for Nutrition Education and Co-Chair of the National Network of Cardiology Dietitians.

While working on Heart and Soul Cuisine, the authors gained a new appreciation for each other's profession. Janice is now ready for chef's school, and David is curious about studying nutrition. Though he may still indulge in foie gras, or dollop whipped cream on fresh berries, Chef Adjey has proven, deliciously, that it is possible to balance elegant gourmet fare with heart-healthy principles.

May 1997

About Healthy Eating

Healthy eating is simply a matter of variety, balance and moderation. This approach may not be very trendy, since it has formed the basis of Canada's Food Guide for years. Yet, if you seriously apply these principles to your everyday food choices, and to your intake of extras like fat, alcohol, caffeine, salt and sugar, I can assure you that they work! You don't need to reach for gimmicks or rely on "too good to be true" promises.

While cutting too much fat from your diet may put you at risk of essential fatty acid deficiency, which can cause skin and hair problems, an extremely high-fat diet puts you at risk of a long list of health concerns, including heart disease and stroke. The message is clear – variety, balance and moderation in food choices form the stepping stones to success. Let's look at each one more closely.

Variety

Webster's Dictionary defines variety as "the absence of monotony or sameness". With the amazing bounty of food surrounding us, we can try foods with new colours, textures and flavours every day. If you restrict yourself to one or two food groups, you will lack more than just variety. By combining foods from all four food groups – meats and alternatives, whole grains, fruits and vegetables and milk products – you're guaranteed important sources of protein, carbohydrate and fibre, not to mention vitamins, minerals and trace elements.

If you've been shying away from trying something new, break out of your shell and go for it! Start with our Garden Greens with Roasted Pepper Toast or a legume recipe like Southwestern Black Bean Soup or Chickpea and Roasted Eggplant Salad. And start making your own low-fat salad dressing, perhaps our versatile Citrus Vinaigrette. Since I started whipping up my own vinaigrettes eight years ago, not once have I gone back to bottled dressings. The flavour is undeniably fresher and more pleasing to the palate. And you must try our colourful flavoured oils! When David and I first discussed the idea of drizzling food with flavoured oil, say basil or cranberry oil, I recall thinking how unusual that sounded. Well, I quickly learned that this simple idea can have a big impact on a recipe's flavour and presentation. For the busy professional, David explains how easy it is to make flavoured oils beginning on page 73.

Balance

Balancing your food intake with the energy you put out is probably a good place to start. If energy in equals energy out, then you'll maintain the balance necessary to control your body weight. There's no question that achieving and maintaining a desired weight is a healthy goal. As you can see by this equation, your activity level is just as important as the amount you eat. If you're not used to any regular form of exercise outside your normal daily activities, start with a simple walk or several short walks for shorter distances instead of relying on transport. You'll be amazed at how much more energetic you feel and how much easier it is in the long run to control your weight and reach other heart-healthy goals. Make sure you have your physician's okay, however, before starting an exercise program. Balancing your food intake entails making the most of all the healthy choices in Canada's Food Guide to Healthy Eating. If you are going to treat yourself to an elegant dinner like our Citrus-Crusted Tuna Steak with Ginger-Green Onion Crepe and Icy Hot Plum Sauce, try lighter fare the next night such as Grilled Eggplant Soup with Vegetable Couscous. The point is clear. Balance meals and snacks higher in fat and sodium with lower fat and sodium choices the next day.

Moderation

"What do you mean by moderation?" is one of the most frequently asked questions about food choices. The best answer is: "Use common sense." Let's review the national guidelines to get an idea of recommended portion sizes and number of daily servings.

CANADA'S FOOD GUIDE TO HEALTHY EATING

Category	Servings
Grain Products	*5-12*
Vegetables and Fruits	*5-10*
Milk Products	*2-4*
Meat and Alternatives	*2-3*

Sample Serving Size

1 slice bread	
3/4 cup cereal	*175 mL*
1/2 cup cooked pasta, potato or rice	*125 mL*
1 medium-sized vegetable or fruit	
1/2 cup fresh or frozen vegetable or fruit	*125 mL*
1 cup milk	*250 mL*
2 ounces cheese	*60 g*
3/4 cup yogurt	*175 mL*
2-4 ounces cooked meat, fish or poultry	*60-120 g*
1 cup beans	*250 g*
1/2 cup tofu	*125 mL*

According to the guidelines, the amount of food you need from the four food groups depends on your age, body size, activity level and whether you're male or female, pregnant or breast-feeding. That's why there's a range within each group. Young children can choose the lower number of servings, while active male teenagers can aim for the highest number. Most people would fall in the middle. So how does your diet measure up? If your serving and portion sizes fit the guidelines, congratulations! If you'd like to cut down on a particular food or drink – like chocolate or alcohol – try the 50% less rule. If you eat a chocolate bar every day, let's say, aim to reduce that bar to one every other day, or to half a bar a day. Your long-term goal might be to treat yourself to one chocolate bar a week, or even one a month. If you want to cut back on alcohol, have two drinks a day instead of four. Over time, aim to cut back to one or two drinks once or twice a week. Remember that everyone is different. That's why it's important to set individual goals that will work for you!

About Change

Change is never easy. And personal habits like eating, exercising, smoking and drinking tend to be the most difficult of all to change. It's these habits, however, that we usually have the most control over.

One of the most common statements I hear from clients and the public is: "If food tastes good, it must be bad for you." Or, when asked what frustrates them most about dieting, they reply, "I can't eat the foods that taste good." As a registered dietitian, my challenge is to convince them otherwise, and to make them feel good about everything they eat. One of the greatest misconceptions is that one high-fat food choice or even an entire day of higher fat meals constitutes failure. Let's face facts and consider just how many meals we actually consume over a lifetime. Between the ages of 2 and 40, we consume over 41,000 meals. I'm sure we'd all like to factor in another 40,000 or more! From this perspective, you can see that over-indulging occasionally will not affect the grand scheme of things. Regardless of age, it's never too late to start making positive changes in your eating habits and lifestyle. You will look and feel better.

But how does one maintain a heart-healthy way of eating from today into the future? After teaching well over 10,000 people about heart-healthy eating during the past 11 years, I've learned that it helps to recognize that we are all at different stages of readiness to change. Research into this phenomenon found that we go through five key stages during the process of change.

Transtheoretical Model Of Change*

1. Precontemplation: "I do not intend to make any changes."
2. Contemplation: "I'm thinking about making changes within the next 6 months."
3. Preparation: "I'm thinking about making changes within the next month."
4. Action: "I have made some changes within the past 6 months."
5. Maintenance: "I've made changes for more than 6 months."

It's normal to get stuck occasionally at a certain stage, or to suffer a relapse. Most of the people I counsel seem to find the contemplation and maintenance stages the biggest hurdles. But once you move into action and reap the psychological and physical rewards of the healthy change, it's easier to use your past experiences to propel yourself forward. I believe that we are far too hard on ourselves. I often see people striving for unrealistic goals that make them feel worse than if they hadn't set any goals at all. Instead of planning big changes that will last only a few months, think small changes that will last a lifetime.

* Changing For Good by J.O. Prochaska, J.C. Norcross and C.C. DiClemente, published by William Morrow and Co. Inc., 1994.

About Goal-Setting

Time and time again, I teach people the principle of setting SMART goals. S stands for Specific, M for Measurable, A for Achievable, R for Realistic and T for Time. Let's say I'm trying to cut back on the amount of added fat I use. In evaluating my current intake, it looks like I add about 4 tablespoons of fat per day including margarine and oil. So that I don't feel totally deprived of fat, I decide that I will be satisfied with half that amount. My SMART goal, therefore, would go like this:

"Limit total added fats (margarine, butter, oil, salad dressing) to 2 tablespoons per day."

This goal is realistic because it still gives me the equivalent of six teaspoons of fat to use. If I'm over or under one day, I can adjust the next day's amount accordingly. The crucial time element is "per day". Using the SMART principle can make setting goals much more meaningful and personal. Goals are meant to be revisited and revised regularly, so that long-term goals can be broken down into several short-term ones that will seem less over-whelming. Now it's your turn. Think about where you want to start. A good place might be fat and sodium, since that's one of the focuses of this cookbook.

About the Recipes

These recipes come from The Estates of Sunnybrook, whose chefs have been acclaimed for their outstanding creative cuisine.

As you read through the wide selection of recipes, you'll discover that each section has been arranged in order of ease of preparation, from everyday dishes like Grill-Smoked Barbeque Chicken to special-occasion favorites like Tandoori-Roasted Swordfish with Pineapple Relish and Green Cardamom Basmati. You'll also find enough challenging recipes, like the Lobster, Lobster, Lobster! dish featured on the cover, to satisfy the most adven-turous cook.

All of our recipes have been adapted for home use and tested in our kitchens to ensure that everyone can manage them – you don't have to be a five-star chef! We've even been prowl-ing grocery store aisles to ensure that all ingredients are readily available. Although substitutions are given for hard-to-find ingredients like togarashi pepper, we encourage you to try these unusual spices and condiments. They will add exciting new flavours to your favourite dishes.

Each recipe includes a nutrient analysis for calories of energy, grams of total fat and saturated fat plus milligrams of cholesterol and sodium as determined by a Professional Diet Analyzer software program. Nutrient values have been rounded to the nearest whole number. Values of less than 0.5 are shown as "trace". Thus, you can cook with confidence knowing that your finished dish will not only look and taste great, it will also be heart-healthy.

As a rule of thumb, have all your ingredients prepared and ready to go before you start cooking, rather than slicing, trimming and chopping as you go. Organizing your kitchen space and supplies as best as possible alleviates stress, and makes you a better cook.

Cooking at home is a luxury in today's fast-paced society. If you're concerned about healthy living, chances are that you're already striving to adjust the pace of your life to minimize stress and to balance healthy eating with physical activity. As we move into the 21st century, we are realizing more and more the value of relaxation, and the pleasure of sharing a meal with friends in our own home. As you indulge in the wonderful taste sensations created by our chefs, we wish you good food, good times and good health.

About Fat, Cholesterol and Sodium

Fat and salt are traditionally used in recipes to give food flavour. Fat has also been touted for enhancing a food's texture and mouth-feel. Relying on fat and salt, however, can mask the intense and more immediate natural flavours of food and limit the use of other, equally sat-isfying flavour and texture enhancers. And don't forget that fat provides a concentrated source of extra calories.

While eating the occasional rich dessert or salty meal is fine, we'll show you a number of simple ways to prepare delicious foods with minimal amounts of fat and salt.

We'll demonstrate how, for example, to create a flavourful, low-fat salad dressing simply by mixing a sweet fruit or juice, such as apple, with an acid such as white wine vinegar. This method of pairing foods to create exciting new flavours is so easy, we know you'll use it often.

Health and Welfare Canada recommends a minimum of 15% dietary fat for all age groups. The average Canadian's fat intake is around 38%. A heart-healthy goal, however, would be less than 30% fat a day. For the average man, aged 19 to 74 years, the daily fat goal should be 90 grams or less, based on a daily intake of 2300-3000 calories. The average woman, who requires 1800-2100 calories each day, should aim for 65 fat grams or less. This translates to about 30% of calories derived from fat. Most health-conscious adults may be even lower than that, between 45-60 grams of total fat.

Let's use the 65 gram fat total for a woman consuming 2100 calories to see how we arrived at the 30% or less figure. First, multiply the amount of fat – 65 grams – by 9, the number of calories in each gram of fat. Divide that total by total calories, 2100 kcal. This gives you the amount of fat calories over total calories. Multiply by 100 to get the percentage.

Example: (65g x 9cal/g ÷2100 kcal) x 100% = 28%

Now, it's not suggested that you "spend" this 30% daily recommendation entirely on saturated fats such as fatty meats, butter, cheese and coconut oil. Instead, heart-healthy guidelines suggest that less than 10% (20g) of your fat intake should be derived from saturated fat with the other 20% (40g) coming from unsaturated oils and soft margarines such as monounsaturates (olive and canola) and polyunsaturates (corn and sunflower). If you aim to limit your total added fats (oil, salad dressing, margarine) to 2 tablespoons (15 mL) a day, and limit your intake of lean meat, fish and poultry to around 4-6 ounces (120-180 g) a day, equal in size to two decks of cards, you'll be right on target with our guidelines.

The majority of our recipes contain 30% or less of fat calories. If a recipe contains 3 grams fat or less per 100-calorie serving, you know it's a heart-healthy choice. But remember to look at your whole day's worth of meals and snacks, not just one item in isolation. No two days will be exactly alike. If we use the example above, the fat grams can be spread over a day with about 15 grams consumed during the morning, 25 grams in the afternoon and 25 grams during the evening.

In terms of dietary cholesterol, heart-healthy eating means less than 300 milligrams of cholesterol a day. This level is easy to achieve if you follow the above guidelines. For example, there's only about 25 milligrams of cholesterol in 1 ounce (30 g) of lean meat, poultry and fish. In short, it's the portion size you eat and how the food is served that can really pile on the extra fat and cholesterol.

If salt is listed as an ingredient, most of our recipes will suggest using only 1/4 or 1/2 teaspoon (1-2 mL). You'll be absolutely amazed at how wonderful the dishes taste with even this small amount of salt because of the variety of flavour-packed fresh herbs and other seasonings and spices used. A heart-healthy sodium level for most people is 3000-5000 milligrams per day. Most heavy salt users will get double this amount, but your body only needs a small fraction of this, so try to use our many suggested alternatives.

For More Nutrition Information

If you would like more information on Canada's Food Guide to Healthy Eating, copies of the Guide and an accompanying booklet entitled Using the Food Guide are available by writing to Publications, Health Canada, Ottawa ON, K1A 0K9. Or contact your local Public Health Nutrition Department, listed in the Blue Pages of your phone book.

Additional pamphlets on a wide range of heart-health topics, including nutrition, can be obtained by contacting your provincial office of the Heart and Stroke Foundation.

For more in-depth and individualized guidelines, you should see a registered dietitian. Contact the Dietitians of Canada office at 416-596-0857 for the name and phone number of a consulting registered dietitian in your community.

Soups

Grilled Vegetable Broth

Chilled Cherry Soup

Fire-Roasted Onion Soup

Maple-Roasted Butternut Squash Soup

Sweet Potato Vichyssoise

Roasted Corn Chowder

Charred Tomato Gazpacho

Southwestern Black Bean Soup

Grilled Eggplant Soup

Chicken Tortilla Soup

Spicy Turkey Gumbo

Asian Style Noodle Soup with Barbequed Duck

Mushroom Consommé

Lobster Bisque "Cappuccino"

Soups

Our quest for lighter eating has created a generation happy to make a meal out of soup. These marvellous dishes transcend the seasons.

Vegetable purées will thicken if they sit for one or two days, and may require additional stock. Soups that are perfectly seasoned when hot can taste bland after being chilled. Each time you prepare a soup recipe, you will become more familiar with its special qualities and better able to improvise. You may want to substitute vegetables, herbs or garnishes, or add more stock than the recipe calls for.

Feel free to experiment.

GRILLED VEGETABLE BROTH

Serves 8

This full-flavoured soup lends itself well to just about any meal. If you can't find all the vegetables listed here, substitute another or double the quantities of one. For extra flavour, I like to grill the pepper, onion and zucchini before dicing.

8 cups Vegetable Stock*	2 L
pinch of saffron	pinch
1/4 cup chopped tomato	50 mL
1/2 cup diced green pepper	125 mL
1/2 cup diced red onion	125 mL
1/2 cup diced zucchini	125 mL
1/4 cup corn niblets	50 mL
1/4 cup cooked black-eyed peas	50 mL
1/8 teaspoon kosher salt	0.5 mL
1/8 teaspoon black pepper	0.5 mL
1 1/2 tablespoons balsamic vinegar	22 mL
1 tablespoon chopped parsley	15 mL

Combine Vegetable Stock and saffron in a stock pot. Bring to a boil then reduce heat to a simmer. Spray a separate pot lightly with non-stick cooking spray. Quickly sauté tomatoes, peppers, onions, zucchini, corn and black-eyed peas over medium heat until tender, about 5 minutes. Add vegetables to stock and bring back to a boil. Reduce heat to a gentle simmer and cook 15 minutes. Remove from heat and season with salt, pepper and vinegar. Ladle into 8 warm soup bowls and garnish with parsley.

* Recipe page 128

nutrient analysis per serving	Total Energy: 114 calories Fat: 4 g Saturated Fat: 1 g Cholesterol: 0 mg Sodium: 122 mg

CHILLED CHERRY SOUP

The freshest local cherries will always produce the finest result.

4 cups cherries, pitted	*1 L*
4 cups apple juice	*1 L*
1 cinnamon stick	*1*
1/3 cup honey	*75 mL*
2 tablespoons cornstarch	*25 mL*
1 teaspoon lemon juice	*5 mL*
1/2 cup chilled Champagne or white wine	*125 mL*
1/4 cup low-fat yogurt	*50 mL*

Combine cherries, apple juice, cinnamon and honey. Bring to a simmer and cook 30 minutes. Remove cinnamon stick. Dilute cornstarch with a small amount of cold apple juice. Stir into soup to thicken slightly. Simmer soup 10 minutes to cook out the starchy taste. Purée soup in a blender or food processor and strain if desired. Chill thoroughly.
To serve, add lemon juice to taste, stir in Champagne and garnish with yogurt.

nutrient analysis

per serving

Total Energy: 216 calories
Fat: 2 g
Saturated Fat: trace
Cholesterol: trace
Sodium: 16 mg

FIRE-ROASTED ONION SOUP

Serves 8

Roasting the onions adds colour and a real depth of flavour to this soup. Always try to use sweet onions such as Vidalia.

6 large white onions	6
1 teaspoon canola oil	5 mL
1 clove garlic	1
2 apples, peeled, cored and chopped	2
1 sprig thyme	1
1 teaspoon ground coriander seed	5 mL
cayenne pepper to taste	
1/8 teaspoon kosher salt	0.5 mL
1/8 teaspoon black pepper	0.5 mL
1/4 cup apple juice	50 mL
6 cups Vegetable Stock*	1.5 L

Preheat outdoor gas grill to high.

Roast onions until completely black and soft. Set aside and cool. Peel onions and wipe with a tea towel to remove black specks. Roughly chop and reserve.

Heat oil in a large saucepan over medium heat. Sauté garlic until lightly browned, being careful not to burn, about 2 minutes. Add onions, apples, thyme, coriander, cayenne, salt and pepper. Sauté until onions are dark brown, about 20 minutes, then deglaze pan with apple juice. Add Vegetable Stock and bring to a boil. Reduce heat to a simmer and cook 20 minutes. Transfer ingredients to a food processor. Purée until smooth. Return to heat and serve warm.

* Recipe page 128

nutrient analysis per serving	Total Energy: 67 calories
	Fat: 1 g
	Saturated Fat: trace
	Cholesterol: trace
	Sodium: 56 mg

MAPLE-ROASTED BUTTERNUT SQUASH SOUP

Serves 8

After trying this soup, you'll want to double the recipe. Keep in mind that leftovers will freeze nicely.

2 large butternut squash, peeled, seeded and cut in large pieces	*2*
2 tablespoons maple syrup	*25 mL*
1/4 teaspoon kosher salt	*1 mL*
1/4 teaspoon black pepper	*1 mL*
1 teaspoon canola oil	*5 mL*
1 large cooking onion, finely chopped	*1*
2 apples, peeled, cored and chopped	*2*
1/8 teaspoon ground ginger	*0.5 mL*
1/8 teaspoon ground coriander	*0.5 mL*
1/2 cinnamon stick	*1/2*
6 cups Vegetable Stock*	*1.5 L*
1 cup evaporated skim milk	*250 mL*

Preheat oven to 400 F / 200 C.

Toss squash pieces with maple syrup, salt and pepper. Place on a cookie sheet and bake 25 to 30 minutes. Remove from oven and reserve.

Heat oil in a large stock pot over medium heat. Add onions and sauté until translucent, about 3 minutes. Add squash, apples, ginger, coriander and cinnamon. Add Vegetable Stock and bring to a boil. Reduce heat and simmer 30 minutes. Remove from heat, discard cinnamon stick and purée in small batches in a food processor. Strain and return purée to saucepan. Gently warm soup and add evaporated milk, being careful not to boil.

* Recipe page 128

nutrient analysis	Total Energy: 159 calories
	Fat: 1 g
	Saturated Fat: trace
per serving	Cholesterol: 1 mg
	Sodium: 88 mg

SWEET POTATO VICHYSSOISE

Serves 8

This adaptation of the classic Vichyssoise should always be served chilled.

1 teaspoon corn oil	*5 mL*
1/2 cup chopped leek, white only	*125 mL*
1/2 cup chopped carrot,	*125 mL*
1 clove garlic, chopped	*1*
1 sprig thyme	*1*
7 cups Vegetable Stock*	*1.8 L*
1 pound sweet potato, peeled and diced	*500 g*
1/2 pound Yukon Gold potatoes, peeled and diced	*250 g*
1/2 teaspoon black pepper	*2 mL*
1/2 teaspoon kosher salt	*2 mL*
1/4 teaspoon ground nutmeg	*1 mL*
cayenne pepper to taste	
1 bay leaf	*1*
1/2 cup evaporated skim milk	*125 mL*

Heat oil in a saucepan over medium heat. Sweat leeks, carrots, garlic and thyme until leeks are translucent. Add Vegetable Stock, sweet potatoes, potatoes, pepper, salt, nutmeg, cayenne and bay leaf. Bring to a boil. Reduce heat to a simmer and cook until potatoes fall apart, about 30 minutes. Remove bay leaf and transfer soup to a food processor. Purée in small batches until smooth and return soup to saucepan over medium heat. Whisk in evaporated milk and adjust seasoning to taste. Serve well chilled.

* Recipe page 128

nutrient analysis	**Total Energy: 96 calories**
	Fat: 1 g
	Saturated Fat: trace
per serving	**Cholesterol: 1 mg**
	Sodium: 181 mg

ROASTED CORN CHOWDER

Serves 8

Locally grown sweet corn will always produce the best result.

1 teaspoon corn oil	5 mL
2 green onions, diced	2
1 jalapeno pepper, seeded and minced	1
pinch of saffron	pinch
4 cups skim milk	1 L
4 cups Chicken Stock*	1 L
6 ears corn, niblets removed	6
2 large russet potatoes, peeled and diced	2
1 sprig thyme	1
1/4 teaspoon black pepper	1 mL
1/4 teaspoon kosher salt	1 mL
1 1/2 teaspoons chopped fresh coriander	7 mL
3/4 cup evaporated skim milk	175 mL
1/4 cup Roasted Pepper Salsa**	50 mL

Heat oil in a large saucepan over medium heat. Add green onions, jalapeno and saffron and sauté gently until onions are tender, about 5 minutes. Add milk, Chicken Stock, corn, potatoes, thyme, pepper and salt. Bring to a simmer. Continue cooking until potatoes are tender, about 30 minutes. Transfer ingredients to a food processor and blend until smooth. Strain chowder back into saucepan and return to heat. Add coriander and evaporated milk. Serve hot, garnished with Roasted Pepper Salsa.

* Recipe page 128
** Recipe page 158

nutrient analysis per serving	Total Energy: 242 calories Fat: 2 g Saturated Fat: trace Cholesterol: 3 mg Sodium: 235 mg

CHARRED TOMATO GAZPACHO

Serves 8

This variation of the classic Spanish soup is cool and refreshing on a warm summer day.

4 large ripe tomatoes, cut in half	4
4 cups tomato juice	1 L
1 tablespoon tomato paste	15 mL
1 jalapeno pepper, seeded and minced	1
1 tablespoon lime juice	15 mL
1/4 cup vodka	50 mL
1 teaspoon Tabasco sauce	5 mL
1/4 teaspoon kosher salt	1 mL
1/8 teaspoon black pepper	0.5 mL
1 yellow pepper, diced	1
1 small red onion, diced	1
2 ears corn, niblets removed	2
1 small zucchini, diced	1
1/2 cup cooked black beans	125 mL
2 tablespoons chopped fresh coriander	25 mL

Place a sauté pan over high heat. Once pan is very hot, char tomatoes cut-side down until black. Remove from heat and reserve. In a food processor, purée tomatoes with tomato juice and paste. Strain mixture to remove seeds.

Season with jalapeno, lime juice, vodka, Tabasco, salt and pepper. Stir in yellow peppers, onions, corn, zucchini, black beans and coriander. Refrigerate 4 hours or overnight to blend flavours. Serve chilled.

nutrient analysis

per serving

Total Energy: 118 calories
Fat: 1 g
Saturated Fat: 0 g
Cholesterol: 0 mg
Sodium: 586 mg

SOUTHWESTERN BLACK BEAN SOUP

Serves 8

If you make this soup ahead of time, you will notice that it thickens quite a bit. To thin it out easily, add a little vegetable stock when reheating.

1 teaspoon canola oil	5 mL
1 large carrot, chopped	1
1 large onion, chopped	1
2 cloves garlic, chopped	2
2 cups black beans, soaked in cold water overnight and drained	500 mL
8 cups Vegetable Stock*	2 L
1 cup sherry	250 mL
1 jalapeno pepper, seeded and chopped	1
1 red pepper, chopped	1
1 teaspoon ground coriander	5 mL
1 teaspoon ground cumin	5 mL
3 tablespoons fresh coriander, chopped	45 mL
1/4 teaspoon kosher salt	1 mL
1/2 teaspoon black pepper	2 mL
1/4 cup Southern Corn Chow-Chow**	50 mL

Heat oil in a large stock pot over medium heat. Add carrots, onions and garlic and sauté 3 minutes. Add black beans, Vegetable Stock, sherry, jalapeno, red peppers, ground coriander and cumin. Bring to a boil. Reduce heat to a simmer and cook until beans are completely soft, about 1 1/2 hours. Add more stock if needed.

Remove from heat and transfer to a food processor. Purée in small batches until smooth. Return to heat and add fresh coriander, salt and pepper. Serve hot, garnished with Chow-Chow.

* Recipe page 128
** Recipe page 155

This soup contains 8 grams of fibre per serving. A good fibre intake is between 20-30 grams a day.

nutrient analysis

per serving

Total Energy: 287 calories
Fat: 2 g
Saturated Fat: trace
Cholesterol: 0 mg
Sodium: 130 mg

GRILLED EGGPLANT SOUP

Serves 8

Eggplant is a remarkable vegetable that absorbs a wide range of flavours. This soup soaks up the warm flavour of cumin.

2 large eggplants, peeled and sliced 1/2-inch/1cm thick	2
3 onions, cut in half	3
1 tablespoon canola oil	15 mL
2 Yukon Gold potatoes, peeled and diced	2
7 cups Vegetable Stock*	1.8 L
1/2 teaspoon black pepper	2 mL
1 bay leaf	1
1/2 teaspoon ground cumin	2 mL
1/4 teaspoon kosher salt	1 mL

Preheat outdoor gas grill to high.
Grill eggplant and onions until tender, about 5 minutes per side.
Remove from grill and let cool. Dice and reserve in a small bowl.
Heat oil in a large saucepan over medium heat. Sauté eggplant and onion 3 minutes. Add potatoes, Vegetable Stock, pepper, bay leaf and cumin. Bring to a boil and reduce heat to low. Cook until potatoes are soft, about 30 minutes. Remove from heat, discard bay leaf and purée in a food processor. Strain purée back into saucepan and adjust salt. Serve hot.

* Recipe page 128

nutrient analysis per serving	Total Energy: 91 calories Fat: 2 g Saturated Fat: trace Cholesterol: 0 mg Sodium: 49 mg

CHICKEN TORTILLA SOUP

Serves 8

This traditional Southwest soup can be made in stages. Make the tortilla broth up to 3 days in advance and the Tortilla Hay hours before serving. With these two items prepared, the soup comes together in a snap.

Tortilla Broth:

1 teaspoon Tomato Oil*	5 mL

1 large onion, finely chopped	*1*
1 clove garlic, minced	*1*
4 raw corn tortillas (4-inch/10cm), chopped	*4*
1 jalapeno pepper, seeded and minced	*1*
1 teaspoon chili powder	*5 mL*
1/2 teaspoon ground coriander	*2 mL*
1/2 teaspoon ground cumin	*2 mL*
4 cups Corn Broth**	*1 L*
2 cups canned tomatoes with juice	*500 mL*

Heat Tomato Oil in a large saucepan over medium heat. Sauté onions, garlic, tortillas, jalapeno, chili powder, ground coriander and cumin. Sauté until onions are translucent, about 3 minutes. Add Corn Broth and canned tomatoes and bring to a boil. Reduce heat and simmer 30 minutes. Remove from heat and purée. Strain broth and keep warm.

Chicken Garnish:

6-ounce boneless, skinless chicken breast	*180 g*
1/4 teaspoon kosher salt	*1 mL*
1/4 teaspoon black pepper	*1 mL*
lime juice to taste	
1/2 cup Tortilla Hay***	*125 mL*
1/2 bunch fresh coriander	*1/2*
1/2 avocado, peeled and diced	*1/2*

Preheat oven broiler.
While tortilla broth is simmering, place chicken breast between two sheets of plastic wrap on a firm work surface. Gently pound chicken with the flat side of a cleaver until paper thin. Remove chicken from plastic wrap and season with salt, pepper and lime juice. Place on a cookie sheet and broil until cooked through, 3 to 4 minutes per side. Remove from oven and reserve.
At serving time, cut chicken into thin strips and use as a garnish along with Tortilla Hay, coriander sprigs and diced avocado. Serve hot.

* Recipe page 76
** Recipe page 132
*** Recipe page 145

nutrient analysis	Total Energy: 108 calories
	Fat: 3 g
	Saturated Fat: 1 g
per serving	Cholesterol: 17 mg
	Sodium: 267 mg

SPICY TURKEY GUMBO

Serves 8

This gumbo is thickened with filé powder and okra instead of a traditional roux, making it lighter than the classic version.

1 pound boneless, skinless turkey breast, cut in 1/2-inch/1cm cubes	0.5 kg
2 tablespoons Barbeque Spice Mix*	25 mL
1/2 cup each diced green, red and yellow pepper	375 mL
1/2 cup diced celery	125 mL
1/2 cup corn niblets	125 mL
1/2 cup sliced okra	125mL
1/4 cup diced onion	50 mL
6 cups Chicken Stock**	1.5 L
1 tablespoon filé powder	15 mL
1/8 teaspoon kosher salt	0.5 mL
1/2 teaspoon black pepper	2 mL
cayenne pepper to taste	
2 cups cooked long grain rice	500 mL

Preheat oven to 400 F / 200 C.

In a large bowl, toss turkey with Barbeque Spice Mix. Spread seasoned turkey on a cookie sheet lined with parchment paper. Bake 15 minutes.

Heat a large saucepan sprayed with non-stick cooking spray over medium heat. Add peppers, celery, corn, okra and onions. Sauté 5 minutes. Deglaze pan with 1 cup Chicken Stock and continue to cook until almost dry. Add another cup of stock and the filé. Stir until smooth. Add remaining stock and cook about 10 minutes. Add turkey and cook another 10 minutes. Remove from heat and season with salt, pepper and cayenne. Serve over cooked rice.

* Recipe page 144
** Recipe page 128

nutrient analysis	Total Energy: 157 calories
	Fat: 1 g
	Saturated Fat: trace
per serving	Cholesterol: 35 mg
	Sodium: 326 mg

Maple-Roasted Butternut Squash Soup, p.25 Lobster Bisque "Cappuccino", p.35

ASIAN STYLE NOODLE SOUP WITH BARBEQUED DUCK

Serves 8

This soup makes a great meal in itself and will serve 4 as a main course. Miso, a fermented soybean paste, is a staple of Japanese cooking. It is available in many Asian and natural food stores.

Miso Broth

8 cups Chicken Stock*	*2 L*
1 tablespoon sliced fresh ginger	*15 mL*
1 bunch chopped green onions	*1*
1 tablespoon miso paste	*15 mL*

In a large saucepan, combine Chicken Stock, ginger and green onions over high heat. Bring to a boil then reduce heat to a simmer. Cook 20 minutes. Remove from heat, strain and whisk in miso. Return to saucepan and keep hot.

2 cups egg noodles	*500 mL*
1 teaspoon sesame oil	*5 mL*
1 teaspoon crushed chili flakes	*5 mL*
1/4 cup julienned carrot	*50 mL*
1/4 cup sliced green onions	*50 mL*
1/4 cup julienned snow peas	*50 mL*
1/2 cup barbequed duck, slivered, *skin and excess fat removed*	*125 mL*
1 tablespoon rice wine vinegar	*15 mL*
1 teaspoon black sesame seeds (optional)	*5 mL*
8 sprigs fresh coriander	*8*

In a large saucepan, bring salted water to a boil. Blanch noodles in boiling water 3 to 4 minutes or until tender. Drain noodles and coat evenly with sesame oil. Keep warm.
In a large stainless steel bowl, toss chili flakes, carrots, green onions, snow peas, duck and vinegar. Divide noodles and vegetables among 8 warmed soup bowls and ladle boiling miso broth over top. Garnish with sesame seeds and coriander. Serve warm.

* Recipe page 128

nutrient **analysis**	**Total Energy: 96 calories**
	Fat: 3 g
	Saturated Fat: 1 g
per serving	**Cholesterol: 107 mg**
	Sodium: 107 mg

Jambalaya Rice Salad, p.58

MUSHROOM CONSOMME

Serves 8

This is truly a fantastic way to show off your culinary talents. The earthiness of the mushrooms and the richness of the broth lend elegance to a menu. For a dramatic effect, I often serve this soup in a brandy snifter.

2 pounds shredded button mushrooms	1 kg
1 cup chopped onion	250 mL
9 egg whites	9
1/4 cup chopped tomato	50 mL
1 bay leaf	1
1/2 cup chopped celery	125 mL
1/2 cup diced carrot	125 mL
2 cloves garlic, minced	2
2 sprigs thyme	2
1 clove	1
10 peppercorns	10
3 quarts Vegetable Stock*	3 L
1/4 teaspoon kosher salt	1 mL
2 tablespoons brandy	25 mL
4 shiitake mushrooms, slivered	4
2 oyster mushrooms, slivered	2
1/4 cup chopped fresh chives	50 mL

In a large bowl, combine mushrooms, onions, egg whites, tomatoes, bay leaf, celery, carrots, garlic, thyme, clove and peppercorns. Mix thoroughly. Stir into Vegetable Stock and refrigerate 4 hours or overnight.

In a tall narrow pot, slowly heat stock. Stir gently but constantly to prevent particles from burning on the bottom. Just before boiling point, a "raft" will start to form. Stop stirring and reduce heat. As the egg whites coagulate they will clarify the consommé. The broth should bubble gently on the sides and the raft should be firm. Cook, without stirring or boiling, 30 minutes. Remove from heat. Carefully ladle consommé through cheesecloth, trying not to break raft. Season soup with salt and brandy. Divide mushroom and chive garnish among 8 bowls and pour hot consommé over top. Serve.

* Recipe page 128

nutrient analysis per serving	**Total Energy: 80 calories** **Fat: 1 g** **Saturated Fat: 0 g** **Cholesterol: 0 mg** **Sodium: 162 mg**

LOBSTER BISQUE "CAPPUCCINO"

Serves 8

Making a great lobster bisque takes time. Serve it in a glass coffee cup to display your hard work.

1 tablespoon canola oil	15 mL
1 large onion, chopped	1
1 large carrot, chopped	1
4 stalks celery, chopped	4
shells of 2 large lobsters	2
2 cloves garlic, chopped	2
3 tablespoons tomato paste	45 mL
1/4 cup brandy	50 mL
1/2 cup white wine	125 mL
8 cups Fish Stock*	2 L
4 cups water	1 L
1/2 cup long grain rice	125 mL
1 bay leaf	1
2 sprigs fresh thyme	2
1/2 teaspoon black pepper	2 mL
1 cup evaporated skim milk	250 mL
cayenne pepper to taste	
1/8 teaspoon kosher salt	0.5 mL
1 cup 1% milk, foamed for garnish	250 mL
grated nutmeg	

Heat oil in a large saucepan over high heat. Sauté onions, carrots, celery, lobster shells and garlic until caramelized, about 10 minutes. Add tomato paste and continue to cook 5 minutes. Deglaze pan with brandy and wine. Add Fish Stock, water, rice, bay leaf, thyme and pepper. Bring to a boil, then reduce heat to a simmer. Cook 1 to 1 1/2 hours. Remove from heat and discard bay leaf. Transfer to a food processor and purée mixture, including shells, in small batches until smooth. Pass through a strainer lined with cheesecloth, discard shells and return soup to heat. Add evaporated milk and season with cayenne pepper and salt. Heat milk in a small saucepan over medium heat, whisking constantly until it foams. Garnish soup with foamed milk and grated nutmeg.

* Recipe page 129

nutrient analysis per serving	Total Energy: 136 calories
	Fat: 2 g
	Saturated Fat: trace
	Cholesterol: 2 mg
	Sodium: 137 mg

Salads

Vegetable Couscous

Garden Greens with Roasted Pepper Toast

Tabbouleh

Roasted Beet Salad

Orange-Scented Wild Rice Salad

Cucumber Dill Salad

Cobb Salad

Grilled Vegetable Salad

Tri-colour Tomato Salad

Marinated Tomato Salad

Chickpea and Roasted Eggplant Salad

Marinated Mushroom Salad

Spinach Salad with Poached Pears

Warm Roasted Winter Vegetable Salad

Black Bean Salad

Tuscan Potato Salad

Southwest Shrimp Caesar

Warm Mushroom Salad with Goat Cheese

Asian Vegetable Salad

Asparagus, Fennel and Red Onion Salad

Jambalaya Rice Salad

Chicken Tortilla Salad

Green Curry Chicken Pad Thai

Salads

I like the fact that salads are versatile enough to play a variety of roles in a meal. They can be a creative appetizer, they can pair with meat or fish for a main course, or they can cleanse the palate after a sophisticated meal.

To make great salads, you must use great ingredients – fresh greens, varied in taste and texture, fresh herbs and the highest quality oils and vinegars.

Follow these guidelines, be adventurous and don't be afraid to try new ingredients.

VEGETABLE COUSCOUS

Serves 6

Couscous, or Moroccan Pasta, is a small pellet made from semolina flour. It comes from the same durum wheat grain used in many traditional pastas. In many parts of North Africa, couscous is as much a household staple as rice is in Asia.

2 cups Vegetable Stock*	500 mL
1 cup couscous	250 mL
1 small red onion, diced	1
1 clove garlic, minced	1
1 small red pepper, diced	1
1 small yellow pepper, diced	1
1 small zucchini, seeded and diced	1
cayenne pepper to taste	
1/4 teaspoon kosher salt	1 mL
1/4 teaspoon black pepper	1 mL
1/4 cup dry white wine	50 mL
juice of 1 lemon	1
2 tablespoons chopped fresh parsley	25 mL

In a large, shallow sauté pan, bring Vegetable Stock to a boil. Sprinkle couscous over boiling stock, cover and remove from heat. Let steam 10 minutes. Meanwhile, spray a large sauté pan with non-stick cooking spray. Over medium heat, sauté onions, garlic, peppers and zucchini until onions are translucent, about 3 minutes. Season with cayenne, salt and pepper. Deglaze pan with wine and cook until almost dry, about 3 minutes. Remove from heat and place mixture in a large bowl. Add couscous to vegetables and toss with lemon juice and parsley. Serve at room temperature.

* Recipe page 128

nutrient analysis per serving	Total Energy: 151 calories Fat: trace Saturated Fat: 0 g Cholesterol: 0 mg Sodium: 105 mg

GARDEN GREENS WITH ROASTED PEPPER TOAST

Serves 4

Make sure your salad greens are absolutely clean and dry, so the dressing will cling to them. A salad spinner is a big help.

4 slices baguette, toasted	4
1/4 cup Roasted Pepper Salsa*	50 mL
6 cups organic field greens (mesclun mix)	1.5 L
1/4 cup Balsamic Vinaigrette**	50 mL
2 tablespoons chopped fresh chives	25 mL
1/2 small red onion, sliced paper thin	1/2
1 large ripe tomato, seeded and diced	1

Spread toasts with Roasted Pepper Salsa and set aside. In a large mixing bowl, toss greens with Balsamic Vinaigrette and divide among 4 salad bowls. Garnish each salad with chives, onions and tomato. Carefully place 1 pepper toast on the side of each salad and serve.

* Recipe page 158
** Recipe page 64

nutrient analysis

per serving

Total Energy: 139 calories
Fat: 5 g
Saturated Fat: 1 g
Cholesterol: 0 mg
Sodium: 224 mg

TABBOULEH

The nuttiness of bulgar wheat complements the freshness of the other flavours in this salad. Although bulgar is considered a winter staple in the Middle East, tabbouleh is eaten to celebrate the arrival of summer.

1 cup bulgar wheat	250 mL
1 cup warm water	250 mL
2 cups chopped fresh parsley	500 mL
3 ripe tomatoes, diced	3
2 cloves garlic, minced	2
juice and finely chopped zest of 1 lemon	1
1/3 cup Basic Vinaigrette*	75 mL
1 teaspoon black pepper	5 mL
1/2 teaspoon kosher salt	2 mL

Cover bulgar with water to rehydrate, about 20 minutes. Drain off any excess water and allow to cool. Add remaining ingredients. Mix gently but thoroughly. Let stand, covered, at room temperature at least 1 hour to blend flavours. Do not make more than 4 hours in advance or the parsley will discolour.

* Recipe page 63

nutrient analysis	Total Energy: 130 calories
	Fat: 3 g
	Saturated Fat: trace
per serving	Cholesterol: 0 mg
	Sodium: 161 mg

ROASTED BEET SALAD

Serves 6

Roasting beets with the skin on helps retain nutrients that would otherwise be washed away by boiling.

6 medium purple beets, washed thoroughly	*6*
1/2 white onion, thinly sliced	*1/2*
1 tablespoon olive oil	*15 mL*
1/4 cup raspberry vinegar	*50 mL*
1 tablespoon lemon juice	*15 mL*
1 tablespoon finely chopped fresh thyme	*15 mL*
1/4 teaspoon kosher salt	*1 mL*
1/4 teaspoon black pepper	*1 mL*

Preheat oven to 350 F / 180 C.

Place beets in an ovenproof dish or cake pan. Cover with aluminum foil and roast until soft, about 1 hour. Remove from oven and let cool. Peel beets and cut into 1/2-inch/1cm pieces. In a large bowl, combine beets with remaining ingredients. Mix thoroughly. Serve at room temperature.

nutrient analysis per serving	Total Energy: 49 calories Fat: 2 g Saturated Fat: trace Cholesterol: 0 mg Sodium: 137 mg

ORANGE-SCENTED WILD RICE SALAD

Serves 8

Wild rice is not really rice but the seed of an aquatic grass. It contains more protein than ordinary rice and is especially rich in the amino acid lysine.

1/2 cup orange juice	125 mL
1/2 cinnamon stick	1/2
2 cloves	2
1/2 jalapeno pepper, seeded	1/2
1 cup wild rice, cooked*	250 mL
1 cup cooked long grain rice	250 mL
1/4 cup Basic Vinaigrette**	50 mL
1 teaspoon ground coriander	5 mL
2 tablespoons finely chopped carrot	25 mL
2 tablespoons minced onion	25 mL
2 tablespoons each finely chopped red and yellow pepper	50 mL
4 clementines, peeled and segmented	4
1/4 teaspoon kosher salt	1 mL
1/4 teaspoon black pepper	1 mL

In a small saucepan over medium heat, combine orange juice, cinnamon, cloves and jalapeno. Reduce by half, remove from heat and reserve. Remove cinnamon stick. In a large bowl, combine wild rice with remaining ingredients. Strain reduction over salad, mix thoroughly and adjust seasoning. Serve at room temperature.

*Cook wild rice in lots of boiling water about 35 minutes, or until the grains just start to burst.

** Recipe page 63

nutrient analysis per serving	Total Energy: 98 calories
	Fat: 2 g
	Saturated Fats: trace
	Cholesterol: 0 mg
	Sodium: 99 mg

CUCUMBER DILL SALAD

Don't be alarmed by the amount of salt in this recipe. It will drain the cucumbers of any excess water and allow them to absorb more flavour from the other ingredients.

2 large greenhouse cucumbers	2
1 tablespoon kosher salt	15 mL
1/4 cup chopped fresh dill	50 mL
1/2 cup low-fat yogurt	125 mL
1/4 cup finely diced red onion	50 mL
1/4 cup finely diced red pepper	50 mL
1/4 cup seeded tomato, finely diced	50 mL
1/4 cup finely chopped fresh chives	50 mL
1 tablespoon lemon juice	15 mL
1/8 teaspoon black pepper	0.5 mL

Cut cucumbers lengthwise. Using a small spoon, scrape out seeds and discard. Slice cucumbers into desired shape and place in a large bowl. Add salt and toss. Place cucumbers in a strainer over sink and let stand 1 hour. Gently rinse off salt, drain well and place in a clean bowl. Add remaining ingredients. Mix well. Serve at room temperature or slightly chilled.

This recipe was analyzed using only 1/2 teaspoon/2 mL of the salt called for because rinsing off the salt lowers the sodium content significantly..

nutrient analysis

per serving

Total Energy: 61 calories
Fat: 1 g
Saturated Fat: trace
Cholesterol: 2 mg
Sodium: 318 mg

COBB SALAD

Serves 6

The original Cobb Salad was created in 1936 at Hollywood's Brown Derby restaurant by Robert Cobb, proprietor at the time.

2 greenhouse cucumbers, sliced	2
4 large ripe tomatoes, cut in wedges	4
1/2 cup corn niblets	125 mL
1 large red pepper, coarsely chopped	1
1 red onion, coarsely chopped	1
1/4 cup fresh coriander or parsley, coarsely chopped	50 mL
2 tablespoons Basic Vinaigrette*	25 mL
1 small ripe avocado, chopped	1

Combine cucumbers, tomatoes, corn, peppers, onions and coriander in a large bowl. Toss with Basic Vinaigrette and mix thoroughly. Garnish with avocado and serve.

* Recipe page 63

Avocado contributes to the higher fat content in this recipe. Notice the saturated fat content is only 1 gram per serving out of 7 grams total. Most of the fat is monounsaturated.

nutrient analysis	Total Energy: 132 calories
	Fat: 7 g
	Saturated Fat: 1 g
per serving	Cholesterol: 0 mg
	Sodium: 20 mg

GRILLED VEGETABLE SALAD

Serves 4

Serve as an appetizer or as a side dish to a simple meal. Always try to use the freshest vegetables your local market has to offer.

1 red pepper, quartered and seeded	1
1 yellow pepper, quartered and seeded	1
1 small green zucchini, sliced 1/4-inch/0.5cm thick	1
1 small yellow zucchini, sliced 1/4-inch/0.5cm thick	1
1 small eggplant, sliced 1/4-inch/0.5cm thick	1
1 red onion, sliced 1/4-inch/0.5cm thick	1
1/4 cup Balsamic Vinaigrette*	50 mL
2 tablespoons chopped fresh herbs (parsley, oregano, basil, etc.)	25 mL
1 clove garlic, minced	1
1/4 teaspoon kosher salt	1 mL
1/4 teaspoon black pepper	1 mL
1/4 cup black olives	50 mL
1 bunch fresh parsley	1

Heat outdoor gas grill to high.
Lightly spray vegetables with non-stick cooking spray. Grill until tender and nicely marked but not burnt, 3 to 5 minutes per side. Remove vegetables from grill and allow to cool. In a large bowl, toss vegetables with Balsamic Vinaigrette, chopped herbs and garlic. Season with salt and pepper and let stand, covered, at room temperature to blend flavours. Arrange on platter and garnish with olives and parsley.

* Recipe page 64

Of the 6 grams total fat, most is heart-healthy monounsaturated fat from the olives.

nutrient analysis

per serving

Total Energy: 119 calories
Fat: 6 g
Saturated Fat: 1 g
Cholesterol: 0 mg
Sodium: 287 mg

TRI-COLOUR TOMATO SALAD

Serves 4

Tomatillos are related to chilies, eggplant and potatoes. Apart from their taste and appearance, however, they bear no relation to tomatoes at all. Resembling small unripe green tomatoes with paper-like husks, tomatillos are available in Latin markets.

6 ripe tomatillos, husked, cut in wedges	6
2 large ripe red tomatoes, cut in wedges	2
2 large ripe yellow tomatoes, cut in wedges	2
1/4 cup diced onion	50 mL
1 jalapeno pepper, seeded and finely diced	1
1/4 cup chopped fresh coriander	50 ml
1 teaspoon black pepper	5 mL
1/2 teaspoon kosher salt	2 mL
1 teaspoon fresh lemon juice	5 mL
1/4 cup Basic Vinaigrette*	50 mL
4 teaspoons toasted green pumpkin seeds, for garnish	20 mL

In a large bowl, combine tomatillos, red and yellow tomatoes, onions, jalapeno, coriander, pepper, salt, lemon juice and Basic Vinaigrette. Toss gently. Cover and let stand at room temperature at least 1 hour to blend flavours. Divide salad among 4 bowls and garnish with pumpkin seeds.

* Recipe page 63

To cut the total fat by half, simply omit the pumpkin seed garnish.

nutrient analysis	Total Energy: 107 calories
	Fat: 7 g
	Saturated Fat: 1 g
per serving	Cholesterol: 0 mg
	Sodium: 385 mg

MARINATED TOMATO SALAD

Serves 6

Always use the freshest tomatoes available when creating this salad. If vine-ripened tomatoes are not available, it's best to skip this one.

6 large ripe tomatoes, cut in wedges	6
1/4 cup Balsamic Vinaigrette*	50 mL
1/4 cup chopped sundried tomatoes**	50 mL
1/4 cup black olives, pitted and chopped	50 mL
2 tablespoons capers	25 mL
1/4 cup julienned fresh basil	50 mL
1 1/2 teaspoons finely chopped fresh oregano	7 mL
2 tablespoons finely chopped fresh parsley	25 mL
2 cloves garlic, minced	2
1/4 teaspoon kosher salt	1 mL
1/4 teaspoon black pepper	1 mL

Combine all ingredients in a large bowl. Mix gently but thoroughly. Cover and refrigerate 1 hour to blend flavours. Serve salad at room temperature for greatest flavour.

* Recipe page 64
** When working with sundried tomatoes not preserved in oil, soak them in hot tap water until soft, about 3 minutes. This will make cutting much safer and easier.

nutrient analysis

per serving

Total Energy: 64 calories
Fat: 3 g
Saturated Fat: trace
Cholesterol: 0 mg
Sodium: 423 mg

CHICKPEA AND ROASTED EGGPLANT SALAD

Sicilian eggplant is sweeter and less bitter than regular eggplant. You'll recognize it in the market by its round shape and much lighter purple colour.

1 1/2 teaspoons olive oil	7 mL
1 medium Sicilian eggplant, cubed	1
2 cloves garlic, minced	2
2 tablespoons finely chopped fresh oregano	25 mL
1 cup canned chickpeas, drained	250 mL
2 tablespoons chopped fresh parsley	25 mL
1 small red onion, coarsely chopped	1
1 roasted red pepper, coarsely chopped	1
1/4 cup Balsamic Vinaigrette*	50 mL
1/4 teaspoon kosher salt	1 mL
1/4 teaspoon black pepper	1 mL

Heat oil in a medium sauté pan over medium-low heat. Add eggplant, garlic and oregano. Slowly cook, stirring to prevent garlic from burning, until eggplant is tender, about 10 minutes. Remove from heat and transfer to a large bowl. Add remaining ingredients and toss. Let stand at room temperature at least 1 hour to blend flavours.

* Recipe page 64

nutrient analysis

per serving

Total Energy: 154 calories
Fat: 6 g
Saturated Fat: 1 g
Cholesterol: 0 mg
Sodium: 348 mg

MARINATED MUSHROOM SALAD

This full-flavoured dish is made magic by using the best extra virgin olive oil and aged balsamic vinegar you can find. Keep in mind that most marinated salads taste better the next day.

2 pounds brown mushrooms, lightly washed	1 kg
1/2 onion, finely diced	1/2
3 cloves garlic, minced	3
1 tablespoon chopped fresh herbs (rosemary, parsley, thyme, etc.)	15 mL
1 tablespoon lemon juice	15 mL
1/3 cup Balsamic Vinaigrette*	75 mL
1/8 teaspoon kosher salt	0.5 mL
1/8 teaspoon black pepper	0.5 mL

Spray a large sauté pan evenly with non-stick cooking spray and place over medium heat. When hot, add mushrooms. Sauté until lightly browned, about 3 minutes. Add onions and garlic and continue cooking until onions are translucent, about 2 minutes, being careful not to let the garlic burn. Add herbs and deglaze pan with lemon juice. Remove from heat and add Balsamic Vinaigrette. Season to taste with salt and pepper. Let cool to room temperature before serving in a large bowl.

* Recipe page 64

| nutrient analysis per serving | Total Energy: 73 calories
Fat: 4 g
Saturated Fat: trace
Cholesterol: 0 mg
Sodium: 72 mg |
|---|---|

SPINACH SALAD WITH POACHED PEARS

Serves 4

Pears can be poached and refrigerated up to 3 days in advance, making this salad extremely easy to prepare. I find Bosc or Anjou pears best for poaching.

2 pears, peeled, halved and cored	2
2 quarts water, with juice of 2 lemons	2 L
1 cup Simple Syrup*	250 mL
4 cups water	1 L
6 cups spinach, torn	1.5 L
1/4 cup Yogurt and Honey-Lemon Dressing**	50 mL
1/2 red pepper, diced	1/2

Place cored pears in lemon water to prevent discoloration.

In a large saucepan over high heat, combine Simple Syrup and water. Bring to a simmer. Poach pears until slightly tender, about 10 minutes. Remove from poaching liquid and refrigerate until cool. In a large mixing bowl, toss spinach well with Yogurt and Honey-Lemon Dressing. Divide salad among 4 bowls and garnish with diced peppers. Slice pears and arrange half a pear on top of each salad.

* Recipe page 138
** Recipe page 69

nutrient analysis

per serving

Total Energy: 196 calories
Fat: 1 g
Saturated Fat: 0g
Cholesterol: 0 mg
Sodium: 127 mg

WARM ROASTED WINTER VEGETABLE SALAD

Serves 6

Roasting brings out the natural sweetness of winter vegetables. This salad will add brilliant colour to any meal.

2 cups coarsely chopped carrots	500 mL
2 cups coarsely chopped butternut squash	500 mL
2 cups coarsely chopped rutabaga	500 mL
1 medium red onion, diced	1
4 cloves garlic, smashed	4
1 tablespoon maple syrup	15 mL
1/4 teaspoon kosher salt	1 mL
1/4 teaspoon black pepper	1 mL
1/2 teaspoon chopped fresh thyme	2 mL
1/2 teaspoon chopped fresh rosemary	2 mL
1 tablespoon chopped fresh basil	15 mL
1/4 cup Basic Vinaigrette*	50 mL

Preheat oven to 375 F / 190 C.
In a large bowl, combine carrots, squash, rutabaga, onions, garlic, maple syrup, salt and pepper. Spread mixture on a parchment-lined cookie sheet and bake until tender, about 30 minutes. Check frequently to make sure vegetables are cooking evenly and not burning. Remove from oven and transfer vegetables to a large bowl. Mix in fresh herbs and Basic Vinaigrette. Serve warm or at room temperature.

* Recipe page 63

nutrient analysis

per serving

Total Energy: 98 calories
Fat: 3 g
Saturated Fat: trace
Cholesterol: 0 mg
Sodium: 150 mg

BLACK BEAN SALAD

Serves 4

This salad features the earthy flavour of ancho chilies. If you can't find dried, whole chilies, try using a chili powder made from anchos.

1 cup uncooked black beans	250 mL
6 cups Chicken Stock*	1.5 L
1 bay leaf	1
1 dried ancho chili	1
1 clove garlic	1
1/4 cup chopped green onions	50 mL
1/4 cup each diced red and yellow pepper	125 mL
1/4 cup diced onion	50 mL
1/4 cup corn niblets	50 mL
1 jalapeno pepper, seeded and minced	1
1/4 cup chopped fresh coriander	50 mL
1 teaspoon Tomato Oil**	5 mL
2 tablespoons fresh lime juice	25 mL
2 tablespoons cider vinegar	25 mL
1 teaspoon Tabasco sauce	5 mL
1/4 teaspoon Kosher salt	1 mL
1/4 teaspoon black pepper	1 mL

In a large pot, combine beans, Chicken Stock, bay leaf, chili and garlic. Bring to a rolling boil. Cover and remove from heat. Let stand 30 minutes then return to medium-low heat. This is an alternative to soaking beans overnight. Remove cover and gently simmer beans until tender and fluffy, about 1 hour. Add extra liquid if needed so beans do not boil dry before they are cooked.

Drain beans and spread on a cookie sheet to cool. Remove bay leaf, garlic and chili. Once cool, combine with remaining ingredients in a large mixing bowl. Toss thoroughly. Serve at room temperature.

* Recipe page 128
** Recipe page 76

nutrient analysis

per serving

Total Energy: 211 calories
Fat: 2 g
Saturated Fat: trace
Cholesterol: 0 mg
Sodium: 243 mg

TUSCAN POTATO SALAD

Serves 6

The abundance of bold flavours in this Italianate salad makes it a delicious alternative to the popular creamy potato salad.

16 mini red potatoes	16
1/4 cup diced red pepper	50 mL
1/4 cup diced red onion	50 mL
1/4 cup sundried tomatoes, chopped	50 mL
2 tablespoons capers	25 mL
3 cloves garlic, minced	3
1/4 cup Balsamic Vinaigrette*	50 mL
1/4 cup julienned fresh basil	50 mL
1/8 teaspoon kosher salt	0.5 mL
1/8 teaspoon black pepper	0.5 mL

Preheat oven to 400 F / 200 C.

Place potatoes in a large stock pot and cover with cold water. Bring to a boil and simmer until potatoes slip off the end of a small knife, 15 to 20 minutes depending on size of potatoes. Drain and cool. Cut potatoes in half and roast 10 minutes. Remove from oven, cool and reserve.

Heat a sauté pan, sprayed with non-stick cooking spray, over medium heat. Lightly sauté peppers, onions, tomatoes, capers and garlic until tender, about 4 minutes. Deglaze pan with Balsamic Vinaigrette. Combine with basil, salt and pepper in a large bowl. Serve at room temperature or lightly chilled.

* Recipe page 64

nutrient analysis

per serving

Total Energy: 158 calories
Fat: 3 g
Saturated Fat: trace
Cholesterol: 0 mg
Sodium: 226 mg

SOUTHWEST SHRIMP CAESAR

Serves 4

The addition of sautéed shrimp makes this salad a wonderful summer meal.

12 large shrimp, peeled and deveined	12
1 tablespoon Barbeque Spice Mix*	15 mL
1/8 teaspoon kosher salt	0.5 mL
1/8 teaspoon black pepper	0.5 mL
1/4 cup No Egg Caesar Vinaigrette**	50 mL
4 romaine hearts or 1 large head, washed and chopped	

Dust shrimp with Barbeque Spice Mix and toss to coat evenly. Spray a large sauté pan evenly with non-stick cooking spray and place over medium heat. When hot, sauté shrimp until fully cooked but still tender, 1 to 2 minutes per side. Season with salt and pepper. Remove from heat and reserve.

In a large bowl, toss romaine with No Egg Caesar Vinaigrette. Divide among 4 plates and top each with 3 shrimp.

* Recipe page 144
** Recipe page 68

While it's a little concentrated in cholesterol at 166 milligrams per serving, if you serve this salad as a main course, your total cholesterol for the day will likely still fall within the recommended 300 milligrams.

nutrient analysis per serving	Total Energy: 133 calories
	Fat: 4 g
	Saturated Fat: 1 g
	Cholesterol: 166 mg
	Sodium: 532 mg

WARM MUSHROOM SALAD WITH GOAT CHEESE

Serves 4

Treat yourself to a little goat cheese for a delectably creamy dressing.

2 small heads frisée lettuce or white chicory, cored and washed	2
1/4 cup goat cheese, crumbled	50 mL
2 tablespoons finely chopped red pepper	25 mL
1/2 small onion, diced	1/2
1 cup sliced mushrooms (shiitake, oyster, etc.)	250 mL
1 teaspoon chopped fresh thyme	5 mL
1/4 teaspoon kosher salt	1 mL
1/2 teaspoon black pepper	2 mL
1/3 cup red wine	75 mL
2 tablespoons red wine vinegar	25 mL
2 tablespoons chopped fresh chives	25 mL

In a large bowl, toss frisée with cheese and peppers. Set aside. Heat a large sauté pan, sprayed with non-stick pan coating, over medium-high heat. Sauté onions and mushrooms until tender, about 5 minutes. Season with thyme, salt and pepper. Deglaze pan with red wine and vinegar. Pour hot mushroom mixture over greens. Using a pair of tongs, toss salad and divide among 4 salad bowls. Garnish with chopped chives. Serve immediately.

nutrient analysis

per serving

Total Energy: 124 calories
Fat: 5 g
Saturated Fat: 3 g
Cholesterol: 11 mg
Sodium: 303 mg

ASIAN VEGETABLE SALAD

Serves 4

This salad is best when made just before serving. When made in advance, the flavours intensify but the bok choy gets soggy.

1/4 cup Soy Ginger Vinaigrette*	50 mL
1/2 teaspoon black sesame seeds	2 mL
2 tablespoons rice wine vinegar	25 mL
3 heads baby bok choy, cleaned, stalks separated	3
2 tablespoons pickled ginger, sliced	25 mL
1 green onion, sliced	1
1 large carrot, thinly sliced	1
1 teaspoon minced ginger	5 mL
1/2 cup snow peas	125 mL

Heat outdoor gas grill to high.

In a small bowl, whisk together the Soy Ginger Vinaigrette, sesame seeds and vinegar. Reserve.

Lightly grill bok choy until tender, about 2 minutes per side. Remove from heat, let cool and slice thinly. Reserve.

In a large bowl, combine pickled ginger, green onions, carrots, ginger and snow peas. Add vinaigrette and mix well. Divide salad among 4 bowls. Serve at room temperature.

* Recipe page 66

nutrient analysis

per serving

Total Energy: 59 calories
Fat: 2 g
Saturated Fat: trace
Cholesterol: 0 mg
Sodium: 0 mg

ASPARAGUS, FENNEL AND
CHARRED RED ONION SALAD

Serves 4

This salad combines delicate asparagus, crunchy raw fennel and sweet red onion rings for a beautiful dinner appetizer or luncheon main course.

4 cups lightly salted water	1 L
2 bunches pencil-thin asparagus, trimmed	2
1/4 cup Citrus Vinaigrette*	50 mL
1 medium red onion, sliced into rings 1/2-inch/1cm thick	1
1/4 teaspoon kosher salt	1 mL
1/4 teaspoon black pepper	1 mL
1 large bulb fennel	1

Preheat outdoor gas grill to high.

In a saucepan over high heat, bring salted water to a boil. Blanch asparagus until tender and bright green in colour, 30 to 45 seconds. Remove from water and immediately shock in ice water to stop the cooking process. Drain asparagus, pat dry and transfer to a large bowl with 1 tablespoon/15 mL Citrus Vinaigrette.

Season onion rings with salt and pepper and spray with non-stick cooking spray. Grill over high heat about 2 minutes per side. Transfer grilled onions to bowl with asparagus. Add 1 tablespoon/15 mL vinaigrette and toss lightly, being careful not to break asparagus. Slice fennel paper thin, directly into the bowl, and toss again.

Arrange asparagus, onion rings and fennel on 4 plates and drizzle with remaining vinaigrette.

* Recipe page 65

nutrient analysis per serving	Total Energy: 61 calories Fat: 1 g Saturated Fat: trace Cholesterol: 0 mg Sodium: 174 mg

JAMBALAYA RICE SALAD

Serves 6

This rice salad is a spectacular addition to any buffet table. For best results, I suggest using long grain rice.

1 teaspoon olive oil	*5 mL*
1/4 cup finely chopped carrot	*50 mL*
1/4 cup finely chopped onion	*50 mL*
1/4 cup finely chopped celery	*50 mL*
1/4 cup finely diced red pepper	*50 mL*
2 cloves chopped garlic	*2*
1 ear corn, grilled, niblets removed	*1*
1/2 cup white wine	*125 mL*
9 ripe tomatoes, cored and chopped	*9*
*1 cup Vegetable Stock**	*250 mL*
1 cup long grain rice	*250 mL*
1/4 cup filé powder or sassafras	*50 mL*
Tabasco sauce to taste	
1/4 teaspoon kosher salt	*1 mL*
1/4 teaspoon black pepper	*1 mL*
3 tablespoons fresh lemon juice	*45 mL*
12 baby clams, cleaned	*12*
12 mussels, cleaned	*12*
12 medium shrimp, peeled and deveined	*12*
3 tablespoons chopped fresh coriander	*45 mL*
1 tablespoon chopped fresh chives	*15 mL*

Heat oil in a saucepan over medium heat. Sauté carrots, onions, celery, peppers, garlic and corn until tender, about 4 minutes. Deglaze pan with white wine, reduce until almost dry and add tomatoes, Vegetable Stock and rice. Bring to a boil, reduce heat and simmer until rice is fully cooked, about 18 minutes. Season with filé powder, Tabasco, salt, pepper and lemon juice. Add clams, mussels and shrimp. Continue cooking over low heat until seafood is cooked through, stirring constantly to prevent sticking, about 10 minutes. Discard any unopened clams or mussels and fold in chopped coriander. Serve warm or at room temperature. Garnish with chopped chives.

* Recipe page 128

nutrient analysis	Total Energy: 259 calories
	Fat: 3 g
	Saturated Fat: trace
per serving	Cholesterol: 125 mg
	Sodium: 342 mg

CHICKEN TORTILLA SALAD

Serves 4

Assemble this salad at the last minute to keep tortillas as crisp as possible.

8-ounce boneless, skinless chicken breast	*250 g*
1 teaspoon Barbeque Spice Mix*	*5 mL*
2 heads frisée lettuce, cleaned, leaves separated	*2*
3/4 cup low-fat prepared buttermilk or ranch dressing	*175 mL*
1/2 small red onion, julienned	*1/2*
1 small red pepper, julienned	*1*
1/4 cup fresh coriander leaves	*50 mL*
1 tablespoon lemon juice	*15 mL*
1/4 teaspoon kosher salt	*1 mL*
1/4 teaspoon black pepper	*1 mL*
1/2 cup Tortilla Hay**	*125 mL*

Preheat oven broiler.

Lay chicken breast between two pieces of plastic wrap. Lightly pound chicken on a firm work surface until flattened to about 1/4-inch/0.5cm. Spray chicken with non-stick cooking spray, season with Barbeque Spice Mix and bake on a parchment-lined cookie sheet until cooked through, 3 to 4 minutes per side. Remove chicken from oven, let cool and slice in thin strips. In a large bowl, toss frisée with dressing, onions, peppers, coriander, lemon juice, salt, pepper and chicken. At the last minute, toss in Tortilla Hay. Serve immediately.

* Recipe page 144
** Recipe page 145

nutrient analysis	Total Energy: 201 calories
	Fat: 2 g
	Saturated Fat: trace
per serving	Cholesterol: 34 mg
	Sodium: 749 mg

GREEN CURRY CHICKEN PAD THAI

Serves 4

I enjoy taking the traditional elements of Pad Thai, Thailand's national dish, and transforming them into this delicious variation.

1/2 teaspoon sesame oil	2 mL
8-ounce boneless, skinless chicken breast, sliced thinly	250 g
1/4 cup each julienned red and yellow pepper	125 mL
1/4 cup thinly sliced carrot	50 mL
1/4 cup bamboo shoots	50 mL
1/2 medium onion, sliced thinly	1/2
1/4 cup chopped fresh coriander	50 mL
1/4 cup snow pea shoots or snow peas	50 mL
2 tablespoons rice wine vinegar	25 mL
1 cup Green Curry*	250 mL
3 cups dry rice noodles, softened**	750 mL
1/8 teaspoon kosher salt	0.5 mL
1/8 teaspoon black pepper	0.5 mL
2 cups bean sprouts	500 mL
2 limes, cut in wedges	2

Heat oil in a large sauté pan over medium-high heat. Quickly sauté chicken, then add peppers, carrots, bamboo shoots, onions, coriander and pea shoots. Cook briefly and deglaze pan with vinegar. Reduce heat and add Green Curry and noodles. Continue to sauté until all ingredients are thoroughly mixed and noodles are tender. Remove from heat and season with salt and pepper. Refrigerate until chilled. This salad is best served at room temperature, garnished with bean sprouts and lime wedges.

* Recipe page 62
** Place rice noodles in a large bowl and add enough warm water to cover. Let stand until soft, about 20 minutes. Drain and cover tightly until ready to use.

nutrient analysis per serving

Total Energy: 201 calories
Fat: 2 g
Saturated Fat: trace
Cholesterol: 34 mg
Sodium: 228 mg

Vinaigrettes and Dressings

Basic Vinaigrette

Balsamic Vinaigrette

Emulsified Vinaigrette

Citrus Vinaigrette

Low-Fat Blue Cheese Dressing

Soy Ginger Vinaigrette

Tarragon Dressing

Roasted Corn-Saffron Vinaigrette

No Egg Caesar Vinaigrette

Yogurt and Honey-Lemon Dressing

Parsley Vinaigrette

Mango Vinaigrette

Curry Vinaigrette

Roasted Garlic-Tomato Vinaigrette

Vinaigrettes and Dressings

The traditional oil to vinegar ratio for a classic vinaigrette is three parts oil to one part vinegar. In the following dressings, two-thirds of the oil has been replaced by thickened stock, thus dramatically reducing the fat content.

You'll find that these dressings are excellent not just for salads, but as a way of adding flavour to meat, fish and vegetables without adding excess fat and calories.

Processing the dressing with a blender distributes the small amount of oil through the mixture.

BASIC VINAIGRETTE

Makes 2 cups / 500 mL

Use this recipe as a base, adding any seasonings, herbs and flavours that you enjoy.

*1 cup Vegetable Stock**	*250 mL*
1 teaspoon cornstarch	*5 mL*
1/2 cup white wine vinegar	*125 mL*
1/2 cup extra virgin olive oil	*125 mL*
1/8 teaspoon kosher salt	*0.5 mL*
1/8 teaspoon black pepper	*0.5 mL*

In a small saucepan over high heat, bring Vegetable Stock to a boil.
In a small bowl, dilute cornstarch with 1 teaspoon/5 mL cold water. Gradually stir cornstarch mixture into stock, until stock lightly coats the back of a spoon. Remove from heat and allow to cool. Transfer stock to a blender, add vinegar and oil and blend until incorporated. Season with salt and pepper. Serve immediately or cover and refrigerate until needed.

* Recipe page 128

This low-fat dressing has a little more than 1 teaspoon/5 mL of fat in a 2 tablespoon/25 mL serving.

nutrient analysis per serving	**2 tablespoons / 25 mL**
	Total Energy: 67 calories
	Fat: 7 g
	Saturated Fat: 1 g
	Cholesterol: 0 mg
	Sodium: 20 mg

BALSAMIC VINAIGRETTE

Makes 2 cups / 500 mL

Here is another version of the Basic Vinaigrette. It adapts well to just about any salad.

*1 cup Vegetable Stock**	*250 mL*
1 teaspoon cornstarch	*5 mL*
1/2 cup balsamic vinegar	*125 mL*
1/2 cup extra virgin olive oil	*125 mL*
1/4 teaspoon kosher salt	*1 mL*
1/4 teaspoon black pepper	*1 mL*

In a small saucepan over high heat, bring Vegetable Stock to a boil.
In a small bowl, dilute cornstarch with 1 teaspoon/5 mL cold water. Gradually incorporate cornstarch mixture into stock, stirring until stock lightly coats the back of a spoon. Remove from heat and allow to cool. Transfer stock to a blender, add vinegar and oil and blend until oil is incorporated. Season with salt and pepper. Serve immediately or cover and refrigerate until needed.

* Recipe page 128

nutrient analysis	2 tablespoons / 25 mL
	Total Energy: 71 calories
	Fat: 7 g
per serving	Saturated fat: 1 g
	Cholesterol: 0 mg
	Sodium: 39 mg

EMULSIFIED VINAIGRETTE

Makes 2 cups / 500 mL

This dressing keeps relatively well in the refrigerator. If it separates, simply re-emulsify in the blender before serving.

1 teaspoon Dijon mustard	*5 mL*
1 small red pepper, chopped	*1*
1 tablespoon chopped fresh herbs *(thyme, basil, rosemary, etc.)*	*15 mL*
1/2 teaspoon granulated sugar	*2 mL*
*1 cup Basic Vinaigrette**	*250 mL*
2 tablespoons lemon juice	*25 mL*

Green Curry Chicken Pad Thai, p.60

Place Dijon, peppers, herbs and sugar in a blender. Process at high speed. Slowly add Basic Vinaigrette until an emulsion forms.

Add remaining vinaigrette in a slow, steady stream. Occasionally thin the mixture by adding a little lemon juice. Continue until all the vinaigrette and lemon juice have been incorporated. Adjust seasoning if necessary and refrigerate until needed.

* Recipe page 63

nutrient analysis per serving	2 tablespoons / 25 mL
	Total Energy: 38 calories
	Fat: 4 g
	Saturated Fat: trace
	Cholesterol: 0 mg
	Sodium: 12 mg

CITRUS VINAIGRETTE

Makes 1 cup / 250 mL

This vinaigrette lends itself well to simply grilled fish or poultry. As you cut the fruit, reserve all juices and add to the dressing.

1 lemon, peeled and cut in segments	1
1 lime, peeled and cut in segments	1
1 red grapefruit, peeled and cut in segments	1
1 teaspoon pink peppercorns	5 mL
1 teaspoon chopped fresh chives	5 mL
3/4 cup Basic Vinaigrette*	175 mL

Add the lemon, lime and grapefruit segments with juice, pink peppercorns and chives to the Basic Vinaigrette. Let stand at room temperature 1 hour to blend flavours.

* Recipe page 128

nutrient analysis per serving	2 tablespoons / 25 mL
	Total Energy: 64 calories
	Fat: 5 g
	Saturated Fat: 1 g
	Cholesterol: 0 mg
	Sodium: 15 mg

Flavoured Oils, p.73

LOW-FAT BLUE CHEESE DRESSING

Makes 1 cup / 250 mL

Blending this dressing makes just a little blue cheese go a long way.

1 shallot, finely minced	*1*
1/4 cup apple juice	*50 mL*
2 sprigs thyme, finely chopped	*2*
1/3 cup non-fat yogurt	*75 mL*
1/4 cup buttermilk	*50 mL*
1 ounce blue cheese	*30 g*
1 teaspoon apple cider vinegar	*5 mL*
1/2 teaspoon black pepper	*2 mL*

Spray a small sauté pan with non-stick cooking spray. Over medium heat, sweat shallot until translucent. Add apple juice and thyme; reduce by half. Remove from heat and reserve. Combine yogurt, buttermilk and blue cheese in a food processor. Blend until smooth with apple juice mixture. Season to taste with cider vinegar and pepper.

nutrient analysis
per serving

2 tablespoons / 25 mL
Total Energy: 33 calories
Fat: 1 g
Saturated Fat: 1 g
Cholesterol: 3 mg
Sodium: 73 mg

SOY GINGER VINAIGRETTE

Makes 1 cup / 250 mL

3 tablespoons finely grated ginger	*45 mL*
2 tablespoons lime juice	*25 mL*
1/4 cup light or low-sodium soy sauce	*50 mL*
*1/2 cup Basic Vinaigrette**	*125 mL*
1 teaspoon sesame oil	*5 mL*
1 tablespoon orange marmalade	*15 mL*
1 teaspoon sesame seeds, toasted	*5 mL*
cayenne pepper to taste	

Place ginger in a small piece of cheesecloth and squeeze out all the juice. This should produce about 2 tablespoons/25 mL ginger juice. Reserve juice and discard pulp.

Place juice and remaining ingredients in a large bowl. Mix well. Let stand at room temperature 1 hour to blend flavours.

* Recipe page 63

Low-sodium soy sauce helps to keep the sodium level per serving reasonable.

nutrient analysis	2 tablespoons / 25 mL
	Total Energy: 57 calories
	Fat: 4 g
per serving	Saturated Fat: 1 g
	Cholesterol: 0 mg
	Sodium: 311 mg

TARRAGON DRESSING

Makes 1 cup / 250 mL

This is one of the endless fresh herb dressings you can create using the Basic Vinaigrette as a foundation.

*3/4 cup Basic Vinaigrette**	*175 mL*
2 teaspoons chopped fresh tarragon	*10 mL*
2 teaspoons Dijon mustard	*10 mL*
2 drops Tabasco sauce	*2*

Combine all ingredients in a blender or food processor. Purée until smooth.

* Recipe page 63

nutrient analysis	2 tablespoons / 25 mL
	Total Energy: 52 calories
	Fat: 5 g
per serving	Saturated Fat: 1 g
	Cholesterol: trace
	Sodium: 22 mg

ROASTED CORN-SAFFRON VINAIGRETTE

Makes 2 cups / 500 mL

Chipotle peppers are dried, smoked jalapenos. Canned chipotles in adobo sauce are found in specialty food stores.

2 ears sweet corn	*2*
1 small white onion, minced	*1*
pinch of saffron	*pinch*
3/4 cup Basic Vinaigrette*	*175 mL*
1 chipotle pepper, mashed with a fork	*1*
1/2 teaspoon chopped fresh coriander	*2 mL*

Preheat oven to 350 F / 180 C.
Roast corn in the husks 20 minutes. Remove from oven and let cool. Remove husks and any burnt particles with a tea towel. Remove niblets with a knife and reserve. In a small non-stick pan sprayed with non-stick cooking spray, sauté onions and saffron over medium heat until onions are translucent, about 5 minutes. Deglaze pan with 1 tablespoon/15 mL Basic Vinaigrette. Remove from heat and cool. Combine onions, corn, remaining vinaigrette, chipotle and coriander in a large bowl. Mix well and adjust seasoning if necessary.

* Recipe page 63

nutrient analysis per serving	**2 tablespoons / 25 mL** **Total Energy: 41 calories** **Fat: 3 g** **Saturated Fat: trace** **Cholesterol: 0 mg** **Sodium: 11 mg**

NO EGG CAESAR VINAIGRETTE

Makes 1 1/2 cups/ 375 mL

This contemporary version of the classic dressing packs all the original flavour with a fraction of the calories.

1 anchovy fillet or 1/2 teaspoon/2 mL anchovy paste	*1*
2 cloves roasted garlic	*2*
2 tablespoons capers	*25 mL*
1 teaspoon Dijon mustard	*5 mL*

1 teaspoon lemon juice	*5 mL*
1/8 teaspoon black pepper	*0.5 mL*
*1 cup Basic Vinaigrette**	*250 mL*

In a food processor, blend anchovy, garlic, capers, Dijon, lemon juice and pepper until smooth. With motor still running, slowly add Basic Vinaigrette in a thin, steady stream until incorporated.

* Recipe page 63

nutrient analysis **per serving**	**2 tablespoons / 25 mL** **Total Energy: 46 calories** **Fat: 5 g** **Saturated Fat: 1 g** **Cholesterol: trace** **Sodium: 80 mg**

YOGURT AND HONEY-LEMON DRESSING

Makes 1 cup / 250 mL

1/2 cup non-fat yogurt	*125 mL*
3 tablespoons stoneground mustard	*45 mL*
3 tablespoons honey	*45 mL*
1 lemon, zest and juice	*1*
1/4 teaspoon chopped fresh mint	*1 mL*
1/4 teaspoon kosher salt	*1 mL*
1/8 teaspoon black pepper	*0.5 mL*

Combine yogurt, mustard and honey in a large bowl. Add lemon zest, juice and mint. Adjust seasoning with salt and pepper.

nutrient analysis **per serving**	**2 tablespoons / 25 mL** **Total Energy: 40 calories** **Fat: trace** **Saturated Fat: trace** **Cholesterol: trace** **Sodium: 151 mg**

PARSLEY VINAIGRETTE

Makes 1 1/4 cups / 300 mL

*1 cup Basic Vinaigrette**	*250 mL*
1/2 cup chopped Italian parsley	*125 mL*
2 cloves roasted garlic, mashed	*2*

In a large bowl, whisk together the Basic Vinaigrette, parsley and garlic. Add salt and pepper to taste.

* Recipe page 63

nutrient analysis	2 tablespoons / 25 mL
	Total Energy: 55 calories
	Fat: 6 g
per serving	Saturated Fat: 1 g
	Cholesterol: 0 mg
	Sodium: 16 mg

MANGO VINAIGRETTE

Makes 2 cups / 500 mL

1 large ripe mango, peeled	*1*
4 ripe plum tomatoes, quartered and seeded	*4*
1 bunch green onions, trimmed	*1*
*1 cup Basic Vinaigrette**	*250 mL*
2 tablespoons sherry	*25 mL*

Thinly slice mango, tomatoes and green onions. Place in a large bowl. Add Basic Vinaigrette and sherry. Mix well and let stand at room temperature 1 hour to blend flavours.

* Recipe page 63

nutrient analysis	2 tablespoons / 25 mL
	Total Energy: 48 calories
	Fat: 4 g
per serving	Saturated Fat: trace
	Cholesterol: 0 mg
	Sodium: 38 mg

CURRY VINAIGRETTE

1/4 cup finely diced pineapple	*50 mL*
1/2 teaspoon minced jalapeno pepper	*2 mL*
1 teaspoon curry powder	*5 mL*
1 cup Basic Vinaigrette*	*250 mL*
1 tablespoon chopped fresh coriander	*15 mL*

Spray a non-stick pan with non-stick cooking spray. Over medium heat, sauté pineapple and jalapeno 5 minutes then add curry powder. Cook 1 minute longer and remove from heat. Stir in Basic Vinaigrette and coriander and allow to cool. Let stand at room temperature 1 hour to blend flavours.

* Recipe page 63

nutrient analysis	2 tablespoons / 25 mL
	Total Energy: 70 calories
	Fat: 7 g
per serving	Saturated Fat: 1 g
	Cholesterol: 0 mg
	Sodium: 23 mg

ROASTED GARLIC-TOMATO VINAIGRETTE

Makes 2 cups / 500 mL

Garlic should be roasted whole with the papery outer skin intact. I like to wrap the whole head in foil and bake at 350 F/180 C for about 40 minutes, or until soft. It will have a rich, sweet taste without the harsh taste of raw garlic.

*1 cup Basic Vinaigrette**	*250 mL*
8 cloves roasted garlic, roughly chopped	*8*
4 plum tomatoes, peeled, seeded and diced	*4*
1 large shallot, minced	*1*
1 teaspoon chopped fresh oregano	*5 mL*

Mix Basic Vinaigrette, garlic, tomatoes, shallot and oregano together in a large bowl. Let stand at room temperature 1 hour before serving to blend flavours. Store in the refrigerator in an airtight container.

* Recipe page 63

nutrient analysis

per serving

2 tablespoons / 25 mL
Total Energy: 39 calories
Fat: 4 g
Saturated Fat: trace
Cholesterol: 0 mg
Sodium: 38 mg

Flavoured Oils

Basil Oil

Tomato Oil

Ginger Oil

Red Hot Chili Oil

Cranberry Oil

Curry or Cumin Oil

Flavoured Oils

Flavoured oils can be used in as many ways as you can imagine. Substitute a flavoured oil anywhere you might use a regular oil.

Though we all need some fat in our diet, try to make it as unsaturated and flavourful as possible so that every drop counts.

All of the following oils are made from monounsaturated and polyunsaturated fats such as canola, olive and corn oil.

BASIL OIL

Makes 1 cup / 250 mL

This is the only flavoured oil in the book with a limited shelf life. You could easily sub-stitute parsley or chives. Add it to a vinaigrette or splash it on a finished plate to add colour.

2 cups chopped basil, watercress, etc.	*500 mL*
2 cups olive oil	*500 mL*
1/8 teaspoon kosher salt	*0.5 mL*
1/8 teaspoon black pepper	*0.5 mL*

Wash basil, drain and pat dry. Purée with oil until smooth. Season with salt and pepper and pass through a fine strainer. Store in a closed jar in the refrigerator up to 1 week. Keep in mind that the colour will fade over time.

nutrient analysis	**1 teaspoon / 5 mL**
	Total Energy: 19 calories
	Fat: 2 g
per serving	Saturated Fat: trace
	Cholesterol: 0 mg
	Sodium: 6 mg

TOMATO OIL

1 cup tomato paste	*250 mL*
3 cups canola oil	*750 mL*
1 teaspoon chili flakes	*5 mL*

In a heavy saucepan over medium-high heat, cook tomato paste, removing as much moisture as possible without burning. Stir constantly. Add oil and chili flakes and bring to a simmer. Stir constantly to avoid sticking. Cook about 10 minutes, or until oil is dark, clear and all the tomato paste has fallen to the bottom of the pot. Remove from heat and let cool. Ladle oil into a fine strainer to remove any floating particles. Store in a covered container in the refrigerator indefinitely.

Variation: Woody herbs, such as thyme and rosemary, can be added to the oil at the same time as the chili flakes. Rosemary, with its strong flavour, works well with this oil.

nutrient analysis	1 teaspoon / 5 mL
	Total Energy: 40 calories
	Fat: 4 g
per serving	Saturated Fat: 2 g
	Cholesterol: 0 mg
	Sodium: 2 mg

GINGER OIL

1 cup canola oil	*250 mL*
3 tablespoons fresh ginger, peeled and minced	*45 mL*
1 teaspoon powdered ginger	*5 mL*
2 tablespoons Vegetable Stock* or water	*25 mL*

In a saucepan, heat 1 tablespoon canola oil over medium heat. Add fresh ginger and sauté until soft and translucent. Add powdered ginger and continue to sauté 2 minutes. Stir in Vegetable Stock and bring to a boil. Reduce heat and simmer until mixture forms a paste. Remove from heat and stir in remaining oil. Set aside overnight. Strain through a coffee filter or double cheesecloth.

* Recipe page 128

nutrient analysis per serving	**1 teaspoon / 5 mL** **Total Energy: 39 calories** **Fat: 4 g** **Saturated Fat: trace** **Cholesterol: 0 mg** **Sodium: trace**

RED HOT CHILI OIL

Makes 1 cup / 250 mL

1 cup olive oil	250 mL
1 teaspoon chopped fresh chili peppers, such as jalapeno or serrano	5 mL
1 teaspoon crushed dried chilies, such as ancho or poblano	5 mL
1 teaspoon chili powder	5 mL
1/8 teaspoon salt	0.5 mL

In a medium saucepan over low heat, sauté fresh peppers in 1 tablespoon/15 mL olive oil. Continue cooking until soft, about 2 minutes. Remove from heat and add dried chilies and chili powder. Cool, then blend with remaining oil in a food processor until smooth. Let stand at room temperature overnight, then pass through a fine strainer. Season to taste with salt. This oil may be made up to 3 days in advance if refrigerated. Bring to room temperature before using.

nutrient analysis per serving

1 teaspoon / 5 mL
Total Energy: 39 calories
Fat: 4 g
Saturated Fat: 1 g
Cholesterol: 0 mg
Sodium: 8 mg

CRANBERRY OIL

Makes 1 cup / 250 mL

2 cups cranberry juice	500 mL
1/2 cup grapeseed or canola oil	125 mL

In a small saucepan, reduce cranberry juice over medium heat until very syrupy and 1/2 cup/125 mL remains. Blend syrup and oil in a blender or food processor. Refrigerate, tightly covered, up to 1 month.

nutrient analysis per serving

1 teaspoon / 5 mL
Total Energy: 25 calories
Fat: 2 g
Saturated Fat: trace
Cholesterol: 0 mg
Sodium: trace

CURRY OR CUMIN OIL

1 cup olive oil	*250 mL*
3 cloves garlic, chopped	*3*
1 shallot, chopped	*1*
1/4 cup curry powder or ground cumin seed	*50 mL*
1/4 cup Vegetable Stock* or water	*50 mL*
1/8 teaspoon kosher salt	*0.5 mL*

In a small saucepan, heat 1 tablespoon/15 mL olive oil over medium heat. Add garlic and shallots and sauté until soft and translucent. Stir in curry powder and continue to sauté 2 minutes. Deglaze pan with Vegetable Stock and bring to a boil. Reduce heat and simmer until mixture forms a paste. Remove from heat and mix in remaining oil. Set aside overnight. Strain through a coffee filter or double cheesecloth.

* Recipe page 128

nutrient analysis	1 teaspoon / 5 mL
	Total Energy: 40 calories
	Fat: 4 g
per serving	Saturated Fat: 1 g
	Cholesterol: 0 mg
	Sodium: 6 mg

Sides

Rosemary-Roasted Mini Potatoes

Basmati Rice Pilaf

White Bean Purée

Saffron Basil Whipped Potatoes

Sweet Potato Purée

Buttermilk Whipped Potatoes

Green Bean "Pecandine"

Bourbon-Glazed Onions

Pepper-Corn Spinach

Sweet Pea Pancakes

Lemon-Scented Potato Hash

Wild Mushroom Hash

Black Bean Cakes with Coriander

Apple-Pistachio Bread Pudding

Green Cardamom Basmati Rice

Chili-Corn Pudding

Ginger-Green Onion Crepes

Lobster Stuffed Baked Potatoes

Cracked Olive-Tomato Fondue

Sides

Side dishes are designed to complement main courses.

Mix and match these sides and use them as you like.

ROSEMARY-ROASTED MINI POTATOES

Serves 4

If rosemary is not a favourite, try using different herbs to suit your personal taste.

1 clove garlic, minced	1
1 teaspoon canola oil	5 mL
1 tablespoon finely chopped fresh rosemary	15 mL
1 medium shallot, minced	1
1/8 teaspoon kosher salt	0.5 mL
1/8 teaspoon black pepper	0.5 mL
12 mini red potatoes, halved	12

In a small bowl, combine garlic, oil, rosemary, shallot, salt and pepper. Let stand at room temperature at least 1 hour.

Preheat oven to 350 F / 180 C.

Place potatoes in a medium pot with just enough cold water to cover. Bring to a boil over medium-high heat. Remove from heat. Let stand 5 minutes, drain and let cool. Toss with seasoning mix. Arrange potatoes on a parchment-lined cookie sheet and bake 10 to 15 minutes. Serve warm.

nutrient analysis per serving	Total Energy: 193 calories
	Fat: 1 g
	Saturated Fat: trace
	Cholesterol: 0 mg
	Sodium: 90 mg

BASMATI RICE PILAF

Serves 4

Basmati rice has an exceptionally long grain and exotic aroma when cooked that cannot be matched by any other rice.

2 cups Chicken Stock*	500 mL
pinch of saffron	pinch
1 teaspoon canola oil	5 mL
1 large onion, finely diced	1
1 stalk celery, finely diced	1
1 clove garlic, minced	1
1 bay leaf	1
1/8 teaspoon salt	0.5 mL
1 1/2 cups basmati rice	375 mL
1 cup dry white wine	250 mL

Preheat oven to 375 F / 190 C.

Place Chicken Stock and saffron in a large pot over medium high heat. Reduce heat to a simmer and steep saffron until stock is dark yellow in colour.

Meanwhile, heat oil over medium heat in a large heavy saucepan. Add onions, celery, garlic, bay leaf and salt. Sauté 2 minutes, or until onion is tender and translucent. Add rice to pan and sauté for an additional 2 minutes, stirring constantly. Add warm stock and wine and bring to a boil. Cover and place in the oven until all liquid is absorbed, 15 to 17 minutes. Remove from oven, discard bay leaf and keep warm.

* Recipe page 128

nutrient analysis per serving	**Total Energy: 331 calories** **Fat: 1 g** **Saturated Fat: trace** **Cholesterol: 0 mg** **Sodium: 89 mg**

WHITE BEAN PUREE

Serves 8

Olive oil is a must in this recipe. It not only adds flavour, but it helps to develop a silky smooth texture.

1 pound dried white beans, soaked overnight	500 g
1 tablespoon olive oil	15 mL
2 teaspoons minced garlic	10 mL
1 medium onion, diced	1
1 carrot, diced	1
1 cup Chicken Stock*	250 mL
pinch of cayenne pepper	pinch
1/4 teaspoon kosher salt	1 mL
1/4 teaspoon black pepper	1 mL

In a large saucepan, cover beans with 10 cups/2.5 L of cold water and bring to a boil over high heat. Lower heat and simmer about 1 1/2 hours or until tender, stirring occasionally. Remove from heat. Drain beans. In a 12-inch/30 cm sauté pan, heat oil over medium-low heat. Add garlic, onions and carrots and sauté, stirring occasionally, 5 minutes. Be careful not to brown the vegetables. Add cooked beans, Chicken Stock and seasonings to the pan. Simmer gently 5 to 10 minutes, stirring occasionally, or until vegetables are soft and beans are hot. Place bean mixture in a food processor and purée in 1 or 2 batches. Adjust seasoning and serve.

* Recipe page 128

nutrient analysis	Total Energy: 213 calories
	Fat: 2 g
	Saturated Fat: trace
per serving	Cholesterol: 0 mg
	Sodium: 86 mg

SAFFRON BASIL WHIPPED POTATOES

Serves 4

Saffron is the stigma of an Eastern Mediterranean crocus. Because of the labour involved in harvesting, the reddish threads are the most expensive spice in the world.

4 large Yukon Gold potatoes, peeled and quartered	4
3/4 cup evaporated skim milk	175 mL
pinch of saffron	pinch
1 tablespoon Basil Oil*	15 mL
1/4 teaspoon kosher salt	1 mL
1/4 teaspoon black pepper	1 mL

Place potatoes in a pot and just cover with cold, salted water. Bring to a boil, reduce heat and simmer until tender, about 30 minutes. Drain. Put potatoes through a ricer or food mill and reserve. In a small saucepan over low heat, steep saffron in evaporated milk until brilliant yellow. Stir milk into potatoes; add Basil Oil. Season with salt and pepper.

* Recipe page 75

nutrient analysis	Total Energy: 174 calories
	Fat: 3 g
	Saturated Fat: trace
per serving	Cholesterol: 2 mg
	Sodium: 214 mg

SWEET POTATO PUREE

Serves 8

Sweet potatoes lend themselves well to bold flavours such as vanilla, cinnamon and cloves. If you can't find a vanilla bean, substitute 1/2 teaspoon / 2 mL pure vanilla extract.

6 medium sweet potatoes, peeled and quartered	6
2 medium potatoes, peeled and quartered	2
1 tablespoon margarine	15 mL
1/2 cup evaporated milk	125 mL
1 vanilla bean, split lengthwise	1
1/8 teaspoon kosher salt	0.5 mL
1/8 teaspoon black pepper	0.5 mL

In a large saucepan, cover sweet potatoes and potatoes with cold water. Place over high heat and cook until tender, about 30 minutes. In a separate saucepan, melt margarine and add evaporated milk and vanilla bean. Bring to a boil and remove from heat. Let stand 3 minutes. Remove vanilla bean, scrape out seeds, discard bean and return seeds to milk mixture. Drain potatoes and pass through a fine strainer. Stir in milk mixture and season with salt and pepper.

nutrient analysis per serving	**Total Energy: 143 calories**
	Fat: 2 g
	Saturated Fat: trace
	Cholesterol: 1 mg
	Sodium: 84 mg

BUTTERMILK WHIPPED POTATOES

Serves 6

Buttermilk and sour cream supply these potatoes with a tangy richness without adding a lot of extra fat.

6 large Yukon Gold potatoes, peeled and quartered	*6*
1/2 cup buttermilk	*125 mL*
2 tablespoons low-fat sour cream	*25 mL*
1/4 teaspoon kosher salt	*1 mL*
1/4 teaspoon black pepper	*1 mL*
2 tablespoons chopped fresh chives	*25 mL*

Place potatoes in a large pot and just cover with cold salted water. Bring to a boil, reduce heat and simmer until potatoes are tender and slip off a small knife, about 20 minutes. Remove from heat, drain and air-dry 5 minutes. Put potatoes through a food mill or mash by hand. Fold in buttermilk, sour cream, salt and pepper. Fold in chives at the last minute and serve warm.

nutrient analysis per serving	**Total Energy: 131 calories**
	Fat: trace
	Saturated Fat: trace
	Cholesterol: 1 mg
	Sodium: 129 mg

GREEN BEAN "PECANDINE"

When buying green beans, always choose beans with bright colour and no brown or soft spots.

1 pound green beans, trimmed	*500 g*
1 small red pepper, julienned	*1*
1 small yellow pepper, julienned	*1*
1 small red onion, julienned	*1*
2 tablespoons chopped fresh chives	*25 mL*
1/4 teaspoon fresh thyme, finely chopped	*1 mL*
1/4 cup Spiced Pecans*	*50 mL*
1/4 cup red wine	*50 mL*
1/2 cup Chicken Jus**	*125 mL*
1/4 teaspoon kosher salt	*1 mL*
1/4 teaspoon black pepper	*1 mL*

Fill a large pot with water and bring to a boil over high heat. Blanch beans until bright green and tender but not soft, about 3 minutes. Remove beans from water and shock in ice water immediately to stop the cooking process. Drain, pat dry and reserve.

Spray a large sauté pan with non-stick cooking spray and place over medium heat. When hot, sauté peppers and onions until tender, about 2 minutes. Add beans and continue cooking until hot, about 3 minutes. Add chives, thyme and Spiced Pecans then deglaze pan with red wine. Reduce liquid until almost dry. Add Chicken Jus and bring to a boil. Season with salt and pepper and serve.

* Recipe page 146
** Recipe page 141

The 6 grams of total fat per serving is mainly from the Spiced Pecans. Pecans are rich in monoun-saturated and polyunsaturated fat.

nutrient analysis per serving	Total Energy: 346 calories Fat: 6 g Saturated Fat: 1 g Cholesterol: 0 mg Sodium: 153 mg

BOURBON-GLAZED ONIONS

Serves 6

With their caramelized sweetness, these onions work best with veal and pork.

2 cups pearl onions, blanched and peeled	500 mL
1/8 teaspoon kosher salt	0.5 mL
1/8 teaspoon black pepper	0.5 mL
2 tablespoons bourbon	25 mL
2 tablespoons maple syrup	25 mL
1/2 cup Vegetable Stock*	125 mL

Lightly spray a large sauté pan with non-stick cooking spray and place over medium heat. When hot, add onions and slowly cook until lightly golden in colour, about 5 minutes. Season with salt and pepper. Deglaze pan with bourbon, remove from heat so as not to ignite alcohol and reduce until almost dry, about 3 minutes. Add maple syrup and caramelize. Add Vegetable Stock and cook 3 minutes, or until juices begin to thicken and shine.

* Recipe page 128

nutrient analysis per serving	Total Energy: 75 calories
	Fat: trace
	Saturated Fat: 0 g
	Cholesterol: 0 mg
	Sodium: 59 mg

PEPPER-CORN SPINACH

Serves 4

By keeping the cooking time short, you will be able to retain the nutrients found in spinach, such as vitamin A and potassium.

1 teaspoon olive oil	5 mL
1 ear corn, niblets removed	1
1/2 each red and yellow pepper, diced to match size of corn	1
1 small red onion, diced	1
1 clove garlic, minced	1
2 bunches spinach, trimmed	2
1/8 teaspoon Barbeque Spice Mix*	0.5 mL

Heat oil in a large sauté pan over medium heat. Add corn, peppers, onions and garlic. Sauté until tender, 2 to 3 minutes. Add spinach and toss frequently until wilted and dark green in colour, about 4 minutes. Remove from heat and season to taste with Barbeque Spice Mix. Serve warm.

* Recipe page 144

nutrient analysis per serving	Total Energy: 87 calories
	Fat: 2 g
	Saturated Fat: trace
	Cholesterol: 0 mg
	Sodium: 85 mg

SWEET PEA PANCAKES

Makes about 24 silver-dollar-size pancakes / serves 6

Use fresh or frozen peas for a striking green pancake.

1 cup all-purpose flour	*250 mL*
1 tablespoon baking powder	*15 mL*
1/2 teaspoon salt	*2 mL*
1 cup egg substitute	*250 mL*
1 cup evaporated skim milk	*250 mL*
1/2 cup Sweet Pea Purée*	*125 mL*
1/4 cup chopped fresh parsley	*50 mL*
pinch of nutmeg	*pinch*
1/8 teaspoon black pepper	*0.5 mL*

Sift together flour, baking powder and salt. In a large bowl, whisk together remaining ingredients. Fold in flour mixture. Spray a large non-stick pan lightly with non-stick cooking spray. For each pancake, spoon about 2 tablespoons/25 mL batter into the pan. When bubbles form and edges are light brown, flip pancake and leave until fully cooked, 2 minutes. Keep warm and serve as soon as possible.

*For the Sweet Pea Purée:
In a blender or food processor, purée 1 cup/250 mL sweet peas with 1 tablespoon/15 mL hot water until smooth. Strain through a fine strainer. Reserve liquid and discard solids.

nutrient analysis per serving	Total Energy: 152 calories
	Fat: 2 g
	Saturated Fat: trace
	Cholesterol: 2 mg
	Sodium: 523 mg

LEMON-SCENTED POTATO HASH

Serves 6

With its citrus flavour, this recipe works best as a starch for fish such as salmon.

2 large or 4 medium Yukon Gold potatoes, peeled	2-4
6 cups cold water	1.5 L
1/2 teaspoon kosher salt	2 mL
pinch of saffron	pinch
1 cup julienned leeks, white and light green parts only, lightly blanched	250 mL
juice of 1/2 lemon	1/2
zest of 2 lemons	2
1/2 teaspoon chopped fresh lemon thyme	2 mL
1/8 teaspoon black pepper	0.5 mL
1 tablespoon chopped fresh chives	15mL

In a large pot, place potatoes, cold water, 1/4 teaspoon/1 mL salt and saffron over high heat. Bring to a boil and cook about 10 minutes, or until potatoes slip off a knife yet remain firm. Drain and let potatoes air-dry 5 minutes. With a cheese grater, shred potatoes keeping strands as long as possible. Place potato shreds in a large bowl and carefully fold in leeks, lemon juice, zest, thyme, pepper and remaining 1/4 teaspoon/1 mL salt. Spray a small non-stick pan with non-stick cooking spray and place over medium heat. Place 1/4 cup/50 mL potato mixture in pan and gently push down with a rubber spatula. Cook 5 minutes or until golden brown. Carefully flip and continue cooking until crisp and golden. Keep warm until needed. Garnish with chives.

nutrient analysis	Total Energy: 92 calories
	Fat: trace
	Saturated Fat: 0 g
per serving	Cholesterol: 0 mg
	Sodium: 210 mg

WILD MUSHROOM HASH

Serves 4 as a side dish or 6 as a sauce

This woodsy stew makes an excellent sauce or side dish.

1/4 cup each finely diced red and yellow pepper	*50 mL*
1/4 cup finely diced red onion	*50 mL*
1 clove garlic, minced	*1*
2 cups each sliced shiitake, oyster and brown mushrooms	*1.5 L*
1/8 teaspoon kosher salt	*0.5 mL*
1/8 teaspoon black pepper	*0.5 mL*
cayenne pepper to taste	
1 sprig thyme, finely chopped	*1*
1/4 cup red wine	*50 mL*
1/2 cup Chicken Jus*	*125 mL*

Spray a large sauté pan with non-stick cooking spray and place over medium heat. When hot, lightly sauté peppers, onions and garlic about 30 seconds. Add mushrooms, stirring constantly until tender, about 7 minutes. Season with salt, pepper, cayenne and thyme. Deglaze pan with red wine and reduce until almost dry, about 3 minutes. Reduce heat and add Chicken Jus. Bring to a boil and serve.

* Recipe page 141

nutrient **analysis** **per serving**	**Total Energy: 163 calories** **Fat: 1 g** **Saturated Fat: trace** **Cholesterol: 0 mg** **Sodium: 91 mg**

BLACK BEAN CAKES WITH CORIANDER

Makes 24 small cakes / serves 8

The distinctive, earthy flavour of black beans marries well with coriander and garlic.

2 cups cooked black beans*	500 mL
2 tablespoons coarsely chopped fresh coriander	25 mL
1 garlic clove, minced	1
2 tablespoons thinly sliced green onions	25 mL
2 tablespoons corn niblets	25 mL
1/3 cup egg substitute	75 mL
2 teaspoons all-purpose flour	10 mL
1/8 teaspoon kosher salt	0.5 mL
1/8 teaspoon black pepper	0.5 mL

Preheat oven to 250 F / 120 C.

Mash beans with a potato masher. Add coriander, garlic, green onions, corn, egg substitute, flour, salt and pepper. Combine thoroughly. Form bean mixture into flat cakes 1/2-inch/1cm thick and 2 1/2-inches/6cm in diameter.

Spray a sauté pan with non-stick cooking spray and place over low to medium heat. Sauté in batches until golden brown and crispy on both sides. Bake on a parchment-lined cookie sheet for 10 minutes or until cakes are heated right through. Serve immediately.

* Cooking instructions on page 52.

nutrient analysis

per serving

Total Energy: 73 calories
Fat: 1 g
Saturated Fat: trace
Cholesterol: trace
Sodium: 56 mg

APPLE-PISTACHIO BREAD PUDDING

Serves 8

Traditionally made by English housewives to use up stale bread, these puddings have become a well known comfort dessert. Here, I have made a savoury rendition – a perfect accompaniment for pork.

1 large egg	*1*
1 large egg white	*1*
1 cup skim milk	*250 mL*
1 cup evaporated skim milk	*250 mL*
1/2 teaspoon ground cinnamon	*2 mL*
1/4 teaspoon ground nutmeg	*1 mL*
1/4 cup shelled pistachio nuts, chopped	*50 mL*
8 slices day-old egg bread, crusts removed and cut in 1/2-inch/1cm cubes	*8*
1/4 of a fresh apple, peeled and diced	*1/4*
1/4 cup diced dried apple	*50 mL*
1 1/2 teaspoons finely chopped fresh thyme	*7 mL*
1/4 teaspoon kosher salt	*1 mL*
1/4 teaspoon black pepper	*1 mL*

Preheat oven to 350 F / 180 C.

In a small bowl, whisk together the egg, egg white, milk and evaporated milk.

In a large mixing bowl, combine cinnamon, nutmeg, pistachios, bread cubes, fresh and dried apple, thyme, salt and pepper. Mix well. Stir in egg mixture. Spray muffin tin with non-stick cooking spray and pack in the bread mixture. Place muffin tin in a baking pan containing 1/4-inch/0.5cm warm water. Bake until pudding is firm and golden brown on top, about 30 minutes. Serve warm.

nutrient analysis	Total Energy: 150 calories
	Fat: 4 g
	Saturated Fat: 1 g
per serving	Cholesterol: 28 mg
	Sodium: 295 mg

GREEN CARDAMOM BASMATI RICE

Serves 4

Cardamom is an exotic spice from the ginger family, popular in tropical countries such as India and Sri Lanka.

1 teaspoon canola oil	5 mL
1 cup basmati rice	250 mL
1 teaspoon freshly ground cardamom	5 mL
1/4 teaspoon kosher salt	1 mL
1 1/2 cups cold water	375 mL
2 teaspoons Tabasco sauce (optional)	10 mL
1 bunch fresh coriander, finely chopped in a food processor	1

Preheat oven to 350 F / 180 C.

Heat oil in a small saucepan. Add rice, cardamom and salt and lightly toast. Add water and Tabasco and bring to a boil, stirring constantly. Cover and bake 18 minutes or until rice is fluffy. Remove from oven and keep warm. Thoroughly fold in coriander. Serve warm.

nutrient analysis

per serving

Total Energy: 198 calories
Fat: 1 g
Saturated Fat: 0 g
Cholesterol: 0 mg
Sodium: 165 mg

CHILI-CORN PUDDING

Serves 6

This pudding is really just a soft polenta with bold Southwest flavours.

1 teaspoon vegetable oil	*5 mL*
1/4 cup minced onion	*50 mL*
2 cups Vegetable Stock*	*500 mL*
1/2 cup cornmeal	*125 mL*
2 ears sweet corn, grilled, niblets removed**	*2*
1/2 red pepper, lightly grilled, finely diced	*1/2*
1 teaspoon minced jalapeno pepper	*5 mL*
1 tablespoon chopped fresh coriander	*15 mL*
1 teaspoon chili powder	*5 mL*
1/2 cup grated low-fat mozzarella	*125 mL*

Heat oil in a large saucepan over medium heat. Sauté onions until tender and translucent. Add Vegetable Stock, bring to a boil and gradually stir in cornmeal. Cook over low heat, stirring constantly until cornmeal has absorbed all stock, about 20 minutes. Remove from heat; stir in corn, red and jalapeno peppers, coriander, chili powder and mozzarella. Adjust seasoning to taste. Serve hot.

* Recipe page 128
** Save corn cobs and other vegetable scraps to add to your vegetable stock.

nutrient analysis	Total Energy: 152 calories
	Fat: 5 g
	Saturated Fat: 2 g
per serving	Cholesterol: 11 mg
	Sodium: 112 mg

GINGER-GREEN ONION CREPES

Makes 8 large crepes

These crepes are my rendition of traditional Chinese mu shu pancakes.

1/2 bunch fresh coriander	1/2
1 bunch chopped green onions, green part only	1
2 cups 2% milk	500 mL
1 cup egg substitute	250 mL
1 cup all-purpose flour	250 mL
1 bunch green onions, sliced paper thin	1
1/4 cup ginger, peeled and minced	50 mL
1/4 cup each finely diced red and yellow pepper	125 mL
1 tablespoon black sesame seeds	15 mL
3 drops sesame oil	3
1/8 teaspoon salt	0.5 mL
pinch of togarashi pepper or cayenne	pinch

In a food processor, purée coriander, green onions and milk until smooth. Strain. In a large bowl, combine egg substitute and milk mixture. Whisk in flour, sliced green onions, ginger, peppers, sesame seeds and oil, salt and togarashi pepper. Let stand 20 minutes.

Heat a large non-stick crepe pan over medium-low heat. Coat pan with non-stick cooking spray. Pour 1/2 cup/125 mL batter into pan and quickly swirl pan to coat bottom evenly with a thin layer. Let cook 1 minute. Loosen edges and flip. Continue cooking for a few seconds, then remove.

nutrient analysis	Total Energy: 155 calories
	Fat: 4 g
	Saturated Fat: 1
per serving	Cholesterol: 5 mg
	Sodium: 130 mg

Sweet Potato Purée, p.85 Saffron-Basil Whipped Potatoes, p.85 Buttermilk Whipped Potatoes, p.86

LOBSTER STUFFED BAKED POTATOES

Serves 4

Serve these potatoes with beef tenderloin for the ultimate Surf 'n' Turf.

2 large baking potatoes	*2*
1/3 cup lobster meat, chopped (from 1 pound lobster)	*75 mL*
1/4 cup chopped green onions	*50 mL*
1/4 cup red onion, diced	*50 mL*
1/4 cup diced mixed red and yellow peppers	*50 mL*
1/2 cup buttermilk	*125 mL*
1 large Yukon Gold potato, cooked and mashed	*1*
1/8 teaspoon kosher salt	*0.5 mL*
1/8 teaspoon black pepper	*0.5 mL*

Preheat oven to 350 F / 180 C.
Place baking potatoes in oven and bake until fluffy and fully cooked, about 25 minutes. Meanwhile, spray a saucepan with non-stick cooking spray and place over medium-high heat. When hot, add lobster, green and red onions and peppers and sauté until tender, about 3 minutes. Add buttermilk, reduce heat and fold in mashed Yukon Gold. Season with salt and pepper. Remove baked potatoes from oven and carefully cut in half lengthwise. With a spoon, hollow out potatoes and add to lobster mixture. Spoon lobster into hollow shells and return to oven until warmed through, 10 to 12 minutes. Serve hot.

nutrient analysis

per serving

Total Energy: 201 calories
Fat: 1 g
Saturated Fat: trace
Cholesterol: 10 mg
Sodium: 163 mg

Sweet Pea Pancakes, p.89

CRACKED OLIVE-TOMATO FONDUE

Serves 4

As with any tomato-based dish use only the freshest, ripest tomatoes you can find. I like to serve this with simply grilled fish.

2 teaspoons extra virgin olive oil	10 mL
2 shallots, thinly sliced	2
2 cloves garlic, minced	2
1/4 cup black olives, pitted and coarsely chopped	50 mL
1/4 cup chopped sundried tomatoes	50 mL
4 large ripe tomatoes, coarsely chopped	4
1/4 cup white wine	50 mL
1/8 teaspoon kosher salt	0.5 mL
1/8 teaspoon black pepper	0.5 mL
2 teaspoons balsamic vinegar	10 mL
1/4 cup slivered fresh basil	50 mL
1 tablespoon chopped fresh parsley	15 mL

Heat oil in a large sauté pan over medium heat. Sweat shallots, garlic, olives and sundried tomatoes. Once shallots are tender and translucent, add chopped tomatoes and continue to cook 5 minutes. Deglaze pan with white wine and add salt, pepper and vinegar. Fold in basil and parsley. Serve warm.

The 5 grams total fat per serving in this recipe is mostly monounsaturated, derived from the olives and the olive oil.

nutrient analysis

per serving

Total Energy 88 calories
Fat: 5 g
Saturated Fat: trace
Cholesterol: 0 mg
Sodium: 230 mg

Mains

Chili-Charred Flank Steak

Grill-Smoked Barbeque Chicken

Oven-Fried Buttermilk Chicken

Grilled Beef Tenderloin with Spicy Onion Rub

Guava Barbequed Black Tiger Shrimp

Black Tiger Shrimp Cocktail

Texas Game Chili

Veal Medallions with Bourbon Glazed Onions

Ginger-Glazed Chicken Stir-fry

Poached Salmon on a Bed of Warm Fennel and Artichokes

Seared Chicken Breast with Green Bean
"Pecandine" and Stone Fruit Preserve

Pork Loin with Apple-Pistachio Bread Pudding

Steamed Sea Bass with Clams "Casino"

Mediterranean Fish Stew

Traditional Osso Buco

Tandoori-Roasted Swordfish with Pineapple Relish and
Green Cardamon Basmati

Seared Sea Scallops with Black Bean Cakes and Citrus Vinaigrette

Grilled Grouper with a Fricassee of Lobster,
Corn and Roasted Peppers

Citrus-Crusted Tuna Steak with Ginger-Green Onion Crepe
and Icy Hot Plum Sauce

Steamed Florida Red Snapper with Saffron, Tomatoes, Basil and Thyme

Indian Style Chicken Curry

Grilled Atlantic Salmon on Black and Gold Pasta with Japanese Miso and Green Onion Sauce

Lobster, Lobster, Lobster!

Mains

This is an understandably hefty section, containing many substantial dishes that are the "Heart and Soul" of a meal.

The recipes here fall into two categories, from simple one-step meals, such as Chili-Charred Flank Steak and Oven-Fried Buttermilk Chicken, to the more elaborate Tandoori-Roasted Swordfish and Lobster, Lobster, Lobster!

CHILI-CHARRED FLANK STEAK

Serves 6

Here's a quick, easy way to enjoy one of the leanest cuts of beef. The bold Southwest flavour makes it a great accompaniment for black bean salad.

1 1/2 pounds flank steak	*750 g*
1 cup dark beer	*250 mL*
1/2 cup minced red onion	*125 mL*
1 clove garlic	*1*
1/4 cup Barbeque Spice Mix*	*50 mL*

Combine steak, beer, onions and garlic in a dish and marinate up to 3 hours.
Preheat outdoor gas grill to high.
Drain steak well and coat with Barbeque Spice Mix. Grill to desired doneness, remove from heat and let steaks rest 5 minutes. Slice meat thinly across the grain and serve.

* Recipe page 144

nutrient analysis

per serving

Total Energy: 242 calories
Fat: 10 g
Saturated Fat: 4 g
Cholesterol: 47 mg
Sodium: 602 mg

GRILL-SMOKED BARBEQUE CHICKEN

This dish delivers the flavours of true barbeque in a fraction of the time. Remember to save the flavourful stock for another use.

4 chicken legs, skin removed, cut in half	*4*
4 cups Chicken Stock*	*1 L*
2 teaspoons Barbeque Spice Mix**	*10 mL*
1 cup Barbeque Sauce***	*250 mL*
1/2 cup moistened wood chips	*125 mL*

Preheat outdoor gas grill to medium high.
Place chicken and Chicken Stock in a large pot and bring to a boil. Reduce heat and lightly simmer 10 minutes.
Remove chicken from stock, pat dry and lightly coat with Barbeque Spice Mix. Sprinkle wood chips over the coals, arrange chicken on grill and close lid for 5 minutes. Open lid and begin flipping chicken continuously and basting with Barbeque Sauce (about 1 minute between flips), for 10 minutes. When chicken is fully cooked, juices will run clear.

* Recipe page 128
** Recipe page 144
*** Recipe page 140

nutrient analysis

per serving

Total Energy: 254 calories
Fat: 8 g
Saturated Fat: 2 g
Cholesterol: 89 mg
Sodium: 658 mg

OVEN-FRIED BUTTERMILK CHICKEN

Serves 4

The crispy coating of breaded chicken has always been a favourite. With this recipe, I tried to make the flavour and texture as close to fried chicken as possible without fat. Try using this recipe with boneless, skinless chicken breasts to make a satisfying sandwich.

2 pounds skinless chicken pieces	*1 kg*
1 cup buttermilk	*250 mL*
1 cup white breadcrumbs	*250 mL*
1/2 teaspoon finely chopped fresh thyme	*2 mL*
*1 teaspoon Barbeque Spice Mix**	*2 mL*
1 clove minced garlic	*1*
1/2 teaspoon black pepper	*1 mL*

Preheat oven to 400 F / 200 C.

Line a shallow baking tray with aluminum foil and spray with non-stick cooking spray.

Place chicken and buttermilk in a shallow bowl, toss and let stand at least 1 hour.

In a separate bowl, combine breadcrumbs, thyme, Barbeque Spice Mix, garlic and pepper. Mix thoroughly.

One at a time, remove chicken pieces from buttermilk and coat evenly with crumb mixture.

Arrange chicken on prepared tray and bake 45 minutes or until juices run clear.

* Recipe page 144

nutrient analysis	Total Energy: 397 calories
	Fat: 5 g
	Saturated Fat: 1 g
per serving	Cholesterol: 139 mg
	Sodium: 522 mg

GRILLED BEEF TENDERLOIN WITH SPICY ONION RUB

Most marinades contain a fair amount of oil. I think you will find this recipe superior in a number of ways. The tiny amount of oil results in considerably less flare-up when grilling and greater health benefits. The onion-based marinade actually cooks into the steak, adding extra flavour to the beef.

1 large onion, chopped	1
2 cloves garlic, peeled	2
1 tablespoon Barbeque Spice Mix*	15 mL
1/2 teaspoon canola oil	2 mL
1 tablespoon chopped fresh parsley	15 mL
1 teaspoon Worcestershire sauce	5 mL
1/2 teaspoon Tabasco sauce	2 mL
1 teaspoon black pepper	5 mL
4 4-ounce beef tenderloin steaks	500 g

In a food processor, blend onion, garlic, Barbeque Spice Mix, oil, parsley, Worcestershire, Tabasco and pepper until smooth. Coat steaks with marinade. Refrigerate in a covered container 1 hour.

Preheat outdoor gas or charcoal grill to high.

Season steaks with salt and grill to desired doneness. To cook steaks to medium, grill 6 to 8 minutes per side.

* Recipe page 144

nutrient analysis	Total Energy: 199 calories
	Fat: 9 g
	Saturated Fat: 3 g
per serving	Cholesterol: 59 mg
	Sodium: 286 mg

GUAVA BARBEQUED BLACK TIGER SHRIMP

Serves 4

We use guava jam to make this dish more exotic. You could substitute apricot or cherry jam.

8 jumbo black tiger shrimp	500 g
1 tablespoon Achiote Marinade*	15 mL
juice of 1 lime	1
3 tablespoons guava jam	45 mL
1/2 bunch fresh coriander, chopped	1/2

Preheat outdoor gas grill to high.

In a large bowl, marinate shrimps with Achiote Marinade and lime juice for 15 minutes. Be careful not to over-marinate or the acid in the lime juice will "cook" the shrimp.

Remove shrimp from marinade. Gently wipe off any excess marinade. Grill 3 minutes and turn. Brush with jam and continue cooking for another 3 minutes. Remove shrimp, coat with any remaining jam and coriander.

* Recipe page 147

nutrient analysis per serving	**Total Energy: 184 calories** **Fat: 3 g** **Saturated Fat: 1 g** **Cholesterol: 244 mg** **Sodium: 291 mg**

BLACK TIGER SHRIMP "COCKTAIL"

Wow your guests with this colourful tango for the taste buds, festively presented in a margarita glass.

6 large ripe tomatoes	*6*
2 jalapeno peppers, seeded and minced	*2*
2 tablespoons tomato paste	*25 mL*
2 tablespoons lime juice	*25 mL*
1/8 teaspoon Tabasco sauce	*0.5 mL*
1/4 teaspoon Worcestershire sauce	*1 mL*
1 teaspoon chopped fresh coriander	*5 mL*
1/4 teaspoon black pepper	*1 mL*
2 tablespoons diced yellow peppers	*25 mL*
2 tablespoons diced zucchini	*25 mL*
2 tablespoons diced red onion	*25 mL*
1/4 cup cooked black beans	*50 mL*
4 slices fresh lime	*4*
juice of 2 limes	*2*
kosher salt as needed	
*3 servings Guava Barbequed Shrimp**	*3*
*2 cups baked Tortilla Hay***	*500 mL*

Heat a heavy saucepan over high heat. Char tomatoes until blistered and black on the outside. Remove from heat and transfer tomatoes to a food processor. Add jalapenos, tomato paste and lime juice. Purée until smooth. Strain tomato purée to remove any seeds but allow black specks to go through. Season with Tabasco, Worcestershire, coriander, salt to taste and pepper. Stir in peppers, zucchini, onions and black beans. Let stand at room temperature for at least 1 hour. To serve, rim margarita glasses with lime juice and salt, pour "cocktail" into glasses and top with Guava Barbequed Shrimp and Tortilla Hay.

* Recipe page 106
** Recipe page 145

nutrient **analysis** **per serving**	**Total Energy: 226 calories** **Fat: 3 g** **Saturated Fat: 1 g** **Cholesterol: 183 mg** **Sodium: 288 mg**

TEXAS GAME CHILI

Serves 6

Masa, or Mexican corn flour, is made by boiling corn in a lime solution before grinding to improve its nutritional value. Look for Masa in Latin stores. If it's not available, substitute corn flour or all-purpose flour.

1 pound venison meat, coarsely ground or chopped	*500 g*
1 pound rabbit meat, coarsely ground or chopped	*500 g*
1 onion, diced	*1*
1 clove garlic, minced	*1*
2 tablespoons Masa corn flour	*25 mL*
1 cup tomato sauce	*250 mL*
2 cups Chicken Stock*	*500 mL*
3/4 cup dark beer	*175 mL*
1 jalapeno pepper, seeded and minced	*1*
1 tablespoon chili powder	*15 mL*
1 teaspoon cocoa powder	*5 mL*
1 teaspoon Barbeque Spice Mix**	*5 mL*

In a large pot over high heat, sear venison, rabbit, onions and garlic until meat is grey. Add Masa and stir in tomato sauce, stock, beer, jalapeno, chili powder, cocoa, Barbeque Spice Mix and salt to taste. Bring to a boil then reduce heat to a slow simmer. Cook 30 minutes, cover and continue to cook another 45 minutes, stirring frequently. Remove from heat and let cool, covered. For an even better flavour, refrigerate overnight and reheat before serving.

* Recipe page 128
** Recipe page 144

To further reduce sodium, use salt-free or low-sodium tomato sauce.

nutrient analysis

per serving

Total Energy: 265 calories
Fat: 5 g
Saturated Fat: 2 g
Cholesterol: 152 mg
Sodium: 624 mg

VEAL MEDALLIONS WITH BOURBON-GLAZED ONIONS

Serves 4

This simple veal dish is perfect for building an elegant main course. The sweetness of the glazed onions pairs well with the veal.

1 teaspoon olive oil	5 mL
1 shallot, minced	1
3 cloves garlic, minced	3
2 tablespoons finely chopped fresh thyme	25 mL
1/2 teaspoon black pepper	2 mL
1 tablespoon cider vinegar	15 mL
1/4 cup white wine	50 mL
8 2-ounce portions veal tenderloin	500 g
1/2 teaspoon kosher salt	2 mL
1 recipe Bourbon-Glazed Onions*	1

In a bowl, combine oil, shallots, garlic, thyme, pepper, vinegar and wine. Blend well. Place veal in the marinade and coat evenly. Cover and marinate 1 hour.

In a non-stick pan sprayed with non-stick cooking spray, sear medallions over medium heat to desired doneness, about 3 minutes per side for medium. Remove from pan and reserve. Transfer veal to 4 warm dinner plates, top with Bourbon-Glazed Onions and serve with steamed asparagus.

* Recipe page 88

nutrient analysis

per serving

Total Energy: 274 calories
Fat: 9 g
Saturated Fat: 2 g
Cholesterol: 128 mg
Sodium: 399 mg

GINGER-GLAZED CHICKEN STIR-FRY

Serves 4

2 tablespoons ginger, peeled and minced	25 mL
1 bunch green onions, cut in 2-inch pieces	1
3 cloves garlic, peeled	3
1/2 cup Chicken Stock*	125 mL
1 teaspoon cornstarch	5 mL
1 1/2 tablespoons low-sodium soy sauce	22 mL
1 1/2 tablespoons oyster sauce	22 mL
1 tablespoon sherry	15 mL
1 teaspoon granulated sugar	5 mL
1 teaspoon sesame oil	5 mL
1 tablespoon canola oil	15 mL
1 pound boneless, skinless chicken breast	500 g
2 cups thinly sliced vegetables (bell peppers, carrots, bamboo shoots, etc.)	500mL

Preheat wok or heavy saucepan over high heat.

Combine ginger, green onions and garlic in a small bowl. Reserve.

Combine 1 tablespoon/15 mL Chicken Stock and cornstarch in a small bowl and stir to form a smooth paste. Set aside.

Combine remaining stock, soy sauce, oyster sauce, sherry and sugar in a small bowl. Reserve sauce.

Swirl oils around inside of wok. Add ginger mixture and cook 15 seconds. Add chicken and vegetables and stir-fry 2 minutes. Add sauce and continue to cook 2 minutes more. Stir in cornstarch mixture, bring to a boil and serve.

*Recipe page 128

nutrient analysis per serving	Total Energy: 231 calories Fat: 6 g Saturated Fat: 1 g Cholesterol: 66 mg Sodium: 447 mg

POACHED SALMON ON A BED OF WARM FENNEL AND ARTICHOKES

Serves 4

Artichokes and fennel bring a natural elegance to this dish. The poaching liquid serves as the vinaigrette for the radicchio and frisée salad.

4 4-ounce salmon fillets, pin bones removed	500 g
1/4 teaspoon kosher salt	1 mL
1/4 teaspoon black pepper	1 mL
2 small fennel bulbs, each sliced into 6 rounds	2
8 artichoke hearts, cooked and cut in half	8
1 clove garlic, minced	1
1 teaspoon Tomato Oil*	5 mL
1/4 cup white wine	50 mL
juice of 1 lemon	1
4 cups Fish Stock**	1 L
1/2 bunch fresh parsley, stems removed	1/2
2 heads radicchio, quartered	2
2 small heads frisée lettuce, quartered	2

Season salmon fillets with salt and pepper. Set aside.

Mix fennel, artichokes and garlic. Toss with Tomato Oil. In a hot sauté pan over medium heat, sauté vegetables until lightly browned, 6 to 7 minutes. Deglaze pan with wine, lemon juice and stock. Bring to a simmer and carefully place salmon on top of vegetables. Reduce heat and cover pan with lid or aluminum foil. Poach until salmon is firm to the touch, 5 to 6 minutes. Remove from heat, transfer salmon to a plate and keep warm. Reserve liquid. In the centre of 4 warm dinner plates, place radicchio and frisée. Spoon vegetable mixture over salad and carefully place salmon on top with a little reserved poaching liquid. Garnish with parsley.

* Recipe page 76
** Recipe page 129

Fatty fish like salmon are rich in omega-3 fatty acids. Current research suggests that this type of fat helps to keep the blood thin, thus reducing the risk of blood clots. For this reason, include fish in your diet on a regular basis.

nutrient analysis

per serving

Total Energy: 243 calories
Fat: 9 g
Saturated Fat: 1 g
Cholesterol: 62 mg
Sodium: 374 mg

SEARED CHICKEN BREAST WITH GREEN BEAN "PECANDINE" AND STONE FRUIT PRESERVE

Serves 4

For the last few decades, chicken has been recognized as one of the leanest sources of meat protein. This simple recipe elevates its rather bland taste to flavourful new heights.

4 4-ounce chicken breast supremes	500 g
1 cup apple juice	250 mL
1/4 cup apple cider vinegar	50 mL
1 tablespoon minced shallot	15 mL
1 teaspoon chopped fresh thyme	5 mL
1/4 teaspoon kosher salt	1 mL
1/4 teaspoon black pepper	1 mL
4 servings Green Bean "Pecandine"*	4
1/2 cup Stone Fruit Preserve**	125 mL

Preheat oven to 375 F / 190 C.

In a shallow container, place chicken, apple juice, vinegar, shallots, thyme, salt and pepper. Coat evenly and let stand at room temperature 30 minutes. Remove chicken from marinade and reserve.

Spray a large sauté pan with non-stick cooking spray and place over medium heat. When hot, sear chicken skin-side down until golden brown, about 2 minutes. Flip chicken and sear an additional 2 minutes. Remove chicken from pan and place on a parchment-lined baking sheet. Roast in oven until fully cooked, 8 to 10 minutes.

Divide warm Green Bean "Pecandine" among 4 warm plates. Place chicken on top of beans and finish with Stone Fruit Preserve.

* Recipe page 87
** Recipe page 159

nutrient analysis	Total Energy: 532 calories
	Fat: 8 g
	Saturated Fat: 1 g
per serving	Cholesterol: 69 mg
	Sodium: 377 mg

PORK LOIN WITH APPLE-PISTACHIO BREAD PUDDING

Serves 8

Pork is slowly becoming more popular. Although many still believe it's high in fat, a well-trimmed pork loin is actually quite lean.

8 4-ounce pork medallions	*1 kg*
1/4 teaspoon kosher salt	*1 mL*
1/4 teaspoon black pepper	*1 mL*
1 onion, thinly sliced	*1*
1 clove garlic, minced	*1*
1/2 cup sherry	*125 mL*
2 cups Chicken Jus*	*500 mL*
8 portions Apple-Pistachio Bread Pudding**	*8*

Season pork with salt and pepper. Set aside.

Heat a sauté pan over medium heat. Spray with non-stick cooking spray and sauté pork until lightly browned, about 3 minutes per side. Remove medallions from pan and transfer to a plate. Keep warm.

Return pan to heat and sauté onions until browned, about 5 minutes. Add garlic and cook 1 minute. Stir in sherry and simmer 2 to 3 minutes. Add Chicken Jus, raise heat to high and bring to a boil. Cook until sauce is reduced by half, 8 to 10 minutes.

Arrange medallions on warm dinner plates and spoon sauce over each. Serve with Apple-Pistachio Bread Pudding and vegetables of your choice.

* Recipe page 141
** Recipe page 93

nutrient analysis per serving	Total Energy: 389 calories Fat: 9 g Saturated Fat: 3 g Cholesterol: 118 mg Sodium: 449 mg

STEAMED SEA BASS WITH "CLAMS CASINO"

Serves 6

6 6-ounce sea bass fillets, skin and pin bones removed	1 kg
1/4 teaspoon black pepper	1 mL
1 small onion, minced	1
2 strips smoked bacon, diced	2
2 pounds littleneck clams, washed	1 kg
1 red pepper, finely diced	1
1 yellow pepper, finely diced	1
2 cups Fish Stock*	500 mL
juice of 1 lemon	1
Tabasco sauce to taste	

Season fillets with pepper and reserve.

Heat a sauté pan over high heat. Sweat onions and bacon in pan until onions are translucent, 3 to 4 minutes. Add clams, peppers and Fish Stock. Cover and steam until clams are open, 6 to 8 minutes. Scoop out clams, remove top shells and discard. Reserve bottom halves. Arrange sea bass fillets in pan and cover with aluminum foil. Steam until flesh feels firm, about 8 minutes. Season broth with lemon juice and Tabasco.

Transfer fish to 6 warm rimmed soup bowls. Top with reserved clams and broth.

* Recipe page 129

nutrient analysis per serving	**Total Energy: 423 calories** **Fat: 8 g** **Saturated Fat: 2 g** **Cholesterol: 174 mg** **Sodium: 323 mg**

MEDITERRANEAN FISH STEW

Serves 10

This fragrant dish is a variation on the classic French bouillabaisse.

2 tablespoons olive oil	25 mL
1 medium onion, diced	1
4 cloves garlic, minced	4
1/2 medium green pepper, diced	1/2
1/2 bulb fennel (or 1 stalk celery), diced	1/2
4 medium tomatoes, peeled, seeded and diced	4
1/2 cup tomato juice	125 mL
1/2 teaspoon chili flakes	2 mL
1 teaspoon fennel seed	5 mL
1/2 cup chopped fresh basil	125 mL
3 cups Fish Stock*	750 mL
1 cup dry white wine	250 mL
2 whole Dungeness crabs, cooked, cleaned and cracked	2
1 pound sea scallops	500 g
3/4 pound large shrimp, peeled and deveined	375 g
14 large clams in their shells	14
1 pound boned, skinned white-fleshed fish, cut in 1-inch cubes (halibut, grouper, etc.)	500 g
1 teaspoon kosher salt	5 mL
1/2 cup loosely packed fresh parsley, coarsely chopped	125 mL
10 sprigs oregano	10

Place oil in a large pot over medium heat and add onion and garlic. Cook 4 minutes, or until onion is translucent. Increase heat to high and add peppers, fennel, tomatoes, tomato juice, chili flakes, fennel seed and basil. Cover and bring to a simmer. Reduce heat to medium-low and simmer 12 minutes. Add Fish Stock and wine.

Layer seafood in pot, beginning with crabs, then add scallops, shrimp, clams and fish. Cover and simmer 8 to 10 minutes, or until fish cubes are tender. Do not stir. Taste and add salt if needed.

To serve, ladle stew into large soup bowls. Sprinkle with parsley and oregano.

* Recipe page 129

nutrient analysis per serving	Total Energy: 224 calories
	Fat: 6 g
	Saturated Fat: 1 g
	Cholesterol: 62 mg
	Sodium: 363 mg

TRADITIONAL OSSO BUCO

Serves 4

This recipe is simple and wholesome. Serve with fresh crusty bread for a complete meal.

1 tablespoon canola oil	*15 mL*
4 6-ounce pieces veal shank, about 2 inches/5cm thick	*750 g*
1/8 teaspoon kosher salt	*0.5 mL*
1/8 teaspoon black pepper	*0.5 mL*
2 carrots, finely diced	*2*
3 stalks celery, finely diced	*3*
2 medium onions, finely diced	*2*
3 cloves garlic	*3*
1 cup dry white wine	*250 mL*
1 bay leaf	*1*
Bouquet Garni:	
1/2 bunch parsley	*1/2*
1 sprig thyme	*1*
1 sprig oregano	*1*
1 sprig marjoram	*1*

Preheat oven to 350 F / 180 C.

Heat oil in a large sauté pan over medium heat. Season veal with salt and pepper and brown 3 to 5 minutes per side. Remove from heat and transfer to a large ovenproof casserole dish. Return pan to heat and sauté carrots, celery, onions and garlic until tender and lightly browned, about 5 minutes. Add vegetables to casserole dish. Return pan to heat and add wine. Bring to a boil and scrape bottom of pan to remove any cooked bits. Add wine to casserole with just enough warm water to cover veal. Add bay leaf and Bouquet Garni. Cover dish with aluminum foil and bake 2 hours or until meat pulls away from the bone. Remove from oven. Remove bay leaf and Bouquet Garni. Portion and serve.

nutrient analysis	Total Energy: 369 calories
	Fat: 12 g
	Saturated Fat: 3 g
per serving	Cholesterol: 149 mg
	Sodium: 233 mg

TANDOORI-ROASTED SWORDFISH WITH PINEAPPLE RELISH AND GREEN CARDAMOM BASMATI

Serves 4

More and more people are experimenting with the exotic flavours of India. This dish will give you a great first impression. Look for jars of tandoori paste in the specialty aisle of your supermarket.

2 tablespoons tandoori paste	25 mL
1 teaspoon lime juice	5 mL
1 tablespoon chopped fresh coriander	15 mL
4 6-ounce swordfish steaks	750 g
1 teaspoon kosher salt	5 mL
1 teaspoon black pepper	5 mL
1/4 cup Pineapple Relish*	50 mL
3 cups Green Cardamom Basmati**	750 mL

Preheat oven to 400 F / 200 C.

In a medium bowl, mix together the tandoori paste, lime juice and coriander. Season swordfish with salt and pepper and place in the marinade, coating steaks well.

Spray a large non-stick pan with non-stick cooking spray. Over medium heat, sauté steaks quickly, about 30 seconds a side, being careful not to burn tandoori coating. Remove from pan and transfer to a parchment-lined cookie sheet. Roast 5 minutes or until flesh feels firm. Do not overcook.

Divide Green Cardamom Basmati Rice among 4 warm dinner plates and place swordfish on top. Finish with Pineapple Relish. Serve with vegetables of your choice.

* Recipe page 157
** Recipe page 94

nutrient analysis per serving

Total Energy: 413 calories
Fat: 6 g
Saturated Fat: 2 g
Cholesterol: 67 mg
Sodium: 440 mg

SEARED SEA SCALLOPS WITH BLACK BEAN CAKES AND CITRUS VINAIGRETTE

Serves 4

While some find jicama bland, the crunchy flesh of this bulbous Mexican root is fantastic when paired with citrus.

12 sea scallops, washed and dried	12
1/2 teaspoon Barbeque Spice Mix*	2 mL
1 pound jicama, peeled and cut into matchsticks	1
1 greenhouse cucumber, seeded and cut into matchsticks	1
1 orange, peeled and segmented	1
1 lemon, peeled and segmented	1
1 small grapefruit, peeled and segmented	1
1/4 cup Citrus Vinaigrette**	50 mL
1 bunch watercress	1
4 servings Black Bean Cakes***	4

Preheat outdoor gas grill to high.

In a bowl, toss scallops with Barbeque Spice Mix and grill until firm, about 3 minutes per side. Reserve.

Spray a sauté pan with non-stick cooking spray and place over medium heat. When hot, sauté jicama and cucumber until warm, 1 to 2 minutes. Add orange, lemon and grapefruit segments. Continue to cook until hot. Deglaze pan with Citrus Vinaigrette, remove from heat and reserve.

Divide watercress equally among 4 warm dinner plates. Top with jicama mixture, Black Bean Cakes and scallops.

* Recipe page 144
** Recipe page 65
*** Recipe page 92

nutrient analysis

per serving

Total Energy: 280 calories
Fat: 3 g
Saturated Fat: trace
Cholesterol: 48 mg
Sodium: 320 mg

GRILLED GROUPER WITH A FRICASSEE OF LOBSTER, CORN AND ROASTED PEPPERS

Serves 4

When grilling grouper, begin with a good thick piece so that it remains moist.

4 4-ounce grouper fillets, bones removed	500 g
1 teaspoon kosher salt	5 mL
1 teaspoon black pepper	5 mL
1 large red pepper	1
1 large yellow pepper	1
2 tablespoons diced white onion	25 mL
2 ears sweet corn, cut in niblets	2
1/2 teaspoon chopped garlic	2 mL
1 rock lobster tail, meat removed and chopped	1
1/4 cup dry white wine	50 mL
1 cup Corn Broth*	250 mL
1 bunch fresh coriander or parsley, chopped	1

Preheat outdoor gas grill to high.

Spray grouper with non-stick cooking spray and season with salt and pepper. Let stand at room temperature 30 minutes.

Roast peppers on an open flame until seared black on all sides. Set aside in a covered bowl 15 minutes, then remove skin and seeds. Dice evenly into 1/2-inch/1cm pieces.

Place fillets on hot grill, skin-side up. Grill about 4 minutes. Turn and grill about 3 minutes more or until fish feels firm. Do not overcook. Keep warm.

In a large sauté pan over medium heat, sauté onions until translucent. Add corn, garlic, peppers and chopped lobster meat. Sauté 3 minutes. Deglaze pan with white wine and Corn Broth. Add coriander and adjust seasoning with salt and pepper.

Divide fricassee among 4 warm soup plates and place grouper on top.

* Recipe page 132

nutrient analysis per serving	Total Energy: 338 calories
	Fat: 9 g
	Saturated Fat: 1 g
	Cholesterol: 56 mg
	Sodium: 283 mg

CITRUS-CRUSTED TUNA STEAK WITH GINGER-GREEN ONION CREPE AND ICY HOT PLUM SAUCE

Serves 4

Always demand the freshest sushi-grade tuna when preparing this dish as you will be cooking the fish rare. Tuna stands up well to these bold flavours.

1 teaspoon kosher salt	5 mL
1 teaspoon black pepper	5 mL
1 tablespoon finely chopped jalapeno pepper	15 mL
1 tablespoon finely chopped ginger	15 mL
1 tablespoon chopped fresh coriander	15 mL
3 tablespoons finely chopped lime zest	45 mL
4 6-ounce tuna steaks, 1 1/2-inches/ 3.5cm thick	750 g
1 teaspoon sesame oil	5 mL
1 small bunch gai lan, or Chinese broccoli	1
1 bunch baby bok choy	1
1 cup bean sprouts	250 mL
1 large carrot, krinkle cut	1
1/4 cup Soy Ginger Glaze*	50 mL
1/2 cup Icy Hot Plum Sauce**	125 mL
4 Ginger-Green Onion Crepes***	4

Combine salt, pepper, jalapeno, ginger, coriander and lime zest in a medium bowl. Mix well. Place tuna steaks on work surface and coat well with crust mixture. Let steaks rest 30 minutes at room temperature before cooking.

Preheat a heavy skillet sprayed with non-stick cooking spray and sear steaks 90 seconds a side. Remove from pan and keep warm.

Heat sesame oil in a wok or heavy saucepan over high heat. Stir-fry gai lan, bok choy, bean sprouts and carrots until tender, about 3 minutes. Deglaze pan with Soy Ginger Glaze, remove from heat and divide among 4 warm dinner plates. Place tuna steaks on the stir-fried vegetables. Ladle Icy Hot Plum Sauce over tuna and garnish with rolled Ginger-Green Onion Crepes.

* Recipe page 137
** Recipe page 136
*** Recipe page 96

nutrient analysis

per serving

Total Energy: 443 calories
Fat: 12 g
Saturated Fat: 3 g
Cholesterol: 61 mg
Sodium: 353 mg

STEAMED FLORIDA RED SNAPPER WITH SAFFRON, TOMATOES, BASIL AND THYME

Serves 4

This recipe is ideal for summer, when markets are bursting with wonderful vine-ripened tomatoes.

1/4 cup Fish Stock*	*50 mL*
1/4 cup dry white wine	*50 mL*
pinch of saffron	*pinch*
1/2 teaspoon fresh thyme leaves	*2 mL*
4 6-ounce red snapper fillets, bones removed	*750 g*
1/4 teaspoon kosher salt	*1 mL*
1/4 teaspoon black pepper	*1 mL*
6 plum tomatoes, peeled, seeded and chopped	*6*
1/2 cup fresh basil leaves, loosely packed and slivered	*125 mL*
1 tablespoon Basil Oil**	*15 mL*

In a large saucepan, heat Fish Stock, wine, saffron and thyme over medium heat. Bring to a gentle simmer and cook 5 to 8 minutes. Season fillets with salt and pepper and carefully place in pan. Cover with aluminum foil and steam 5 minutes. Remove foil, gently remove fillets and keep warm. Add tomatoes and basil to pan and cook until just heated, about 3 minutes.

Arrange fillets in warm soup plates. Ladle broth and tomatoes over top. Finish with a drizzle of Basil Oil.

* Recipe page 129
** Recipe page 75

nutrient analysis per serving	Total Energy: 242 calories Fat: 5 g Saturated Fat: 1 g Cholesterol: 62 mg Sodium: 246 mg

INDIAN STYLE CHICKEN CURRY

Serves 4

These Indian flavours are magnificent. I can assure you that, when you take the time to make a traditional curry, you will taste the extra effort. This recipe has been toned down so that the average person can enjoy it. If you prefer a spicier curry, add more cayenne powder.

1 tablespoon ginger, peeled and chopped	15 mL
4 cloves garlic, chopped	4
2 tablespoons curry powder	25 mL
cayenne to taste	
1 1/2 teaspoons ground cumin seed	7 mL
1/2 teaspoon black pepper	2 mL
1/8 teaspoon ground cloves	0.5 mL
1/2 teaspoon ground cinnamon	2 mL
2 cardamom pods, ground	2
1/2 cup coconut water*	125 mL
1 tablespoon canola oil	15 mL
1 medium red onion, sliced	1
1 1/4 teaspoons salt	6 mL
1/2 teaspoon turmeric powder	2 mL
1 1/2 pounds skinless chicken breast, cut in 2-inch/5cm pieces	750 g
3 medium tomatoes, diced	3
2 cups water	500 mL
2 cups cooked basmati rice	500 mL

In a food processor, purée ginger, garlic, curry powder, cayenne, cumin, pepper, cloves, cinnamon, cardamom and coconut water until smooth. Set aside.
Heat oil in a large sauté pan over medium heat. Add onions and cook, stirring, 5 minutes. Stir in salt and turmeric, then add chicken. Stir-fry 10 minutes or until chicken is browned. Add tomatoes, stir and cook 2 minutes, then add water and spice paste. Simmer 20 minutes, or until sauce has thickened and chicken is tender. Serve hot over rice.

*See page 162

nutrient analysis per serving	Total Energy: 418 calories Fat: 7 g Saturated Fat: 1 g Cholesterol: 103 mg Sodium: 423 mg

GRILLED ATLANTIC SALMON ON BLACK AND GOLD PASTA WITH JAPANESE MISO AND GREEN ONION SAUCE

Serves 8

This eclectic dish has changed little since I first saw it at Melrose Restaurant in New York City with chef Richard Krause. Don't be discouraged by the list of ingredients, this dish is well worth the effort and will excite both your eye and your palate.

8 6-ounce salmon fillets, bones removed	1.5 kg
1/8 teaspoon togarashi pepper or cayenne	0.5 mL
2 tablespoons golden Japanese miso*	25 mL
1/2 cup Japanese plum wine or sherry	125 mL
1 tablespoon finely minced ginger	15 mL
1 tablespoon sesame oil	15 mL
1 teaspoon chopped fresh coriander	5 mL
2 bunches green onions, chopped	2
2 egg whites	2
1 1/2 cups rice wine vinegar	375 mL
1/2 cup canola oil	125 mL
1/2 pound fresh saffron spaghetti	250 g
1/2 pound fresh squid ink spaghetti	250 g
2 cups julienned vegetables (carrots, red and yellow peppers, cucumbers, etc.)	500 mL
1/4 cup sunflower seedlings or bean sprouts (optional)	50 mL

Preheat outdoor gas grill to high. Season fillets with togarashi pepper and spray with non-stick cooking spray. Reserve. In a large bowl, whisk together miso, plum wine, ginger, sesame oil and coriander. Reserve. Place green onions, egg whites and rice wine vinegar in a blender. Purée until smooth. With blender running, slowly add oil until incorporated. Grill salmon to desired doneness, about 3 minutes per side. Keep warm. In a large pot of boiling water, cook pasta until al dente, about 3 minutes. Drain and place in a large bowl with miso dressing and vegetables. Toss to mix and divide pasta among 4 warm dinner plates. Top with grilled salmon. Garnish with green onion dressing.

* Miso and togarashi pepper can be found in Japanese and specialty food markets.

A 4-ounce/125 g piece of raw salmon contains 4 to 8 grams of omega-3 fatty acids. The recommended intake of omega-3 fats for men and women aged 19-74 years is 1.1 to 1.6 grams per day.

nutrient analysis per serving	Total Energy: 406 calories
	Fat: 15 g
	Saturated Fat: 2 g
	Cholesterol: 93 mg
	Sodium: 227 mg

LOBSTER, LOBSTER, LOBSTER!

Serves 4

This signature dish is the ultimate indulgence. Due to traditional cooking and serving methods, lobster has always been perceived as a forbidden food. We set out to prove that even the most extravagant meal can be prepared with little fat. Don't be over-whelmed by the number of ingredients — each step is simple and easy to complete.

4 1 1/4-pound lobsters	2.3 kg
1 quart Court-Bouillon*	1 L
3 egg whites	3
5 ounces white fish fillet, cubed and frozen	150 g
1/8 teaspoon salt	0.5 mL
1/2 teaspoon chopped fresh coriander	2 mL
1 tablespoon diced red pepper	15 mL
1 tablespoon corn niblets	15 mL
cayenne pepper to taste	
4 natural sausage casings (optional)	4
dried corn husks for ties	
1 tablespoon corn oil	15 mL
2 cups chopped onions	500 mL
2 cups chopped celery	500 mL
2 cups chopped red and yellow pepper	500 mL
2 tablespoons filé powder	25 mL
1 tablespoon Tabasco sauce	15 mL
1 teaspoon minced garlic	5 mL
1 1/4 cups canned tomatoes with juice	300 mL
5 cups Fish Stock**	1.25 L
24 littleneck clams (2 ounces/60 g meat)	24
1 cup corn niblets (preferably fresh)	250 mL
12 okra pods	12
2 cups Basmati Rice Pilaf***	500 mL
12 Old Bay Breadsticks****	12

Poach lobsters in boiling Court-Bouillon for 2 minutes. Remove and place in ice water to cool. Remove claws and shell, chop meat and reserve. Crack tail, extract, devein and reserve meat. Cut lobster torso in half, crosswise, to use as a base for presentation.

Purée egg whites and fish in a food processor until well mixed, about 3 minutes. Transfer to a bowl. Season with salt and fold in chopped claw meat, coriander, red pepper, corn and cayenne. Stuff mixture into sausage casings. Tie off into links with corn husks. Blanch sausages in simmering water until firm, about 8 minutes, then shock in ice water. Refrigerate.

Heat oil over medium heat in a heavy saucepan. Add onions, celery and peppers. Turn heat to high and stir in filé, Tabasco and garlic. Cook 5 to 6 minutes, stirring constantly. Reduce heat to medium and stir in tomatoes. Continue cooking 5 minutes. Add stock and bring gumbo to a boil. Reduce heat and simmer 1 hour. Add clams and lobster meat and poach 3 to 4 minutes. Then add corn and okra.

Preheat oven broiler.

Broil lobster tails until warmed through, 3 to 4 minutes. Lightly coat a non-stick pan with cooking spray. Sauté sausage over medium-low heat until warmed through.

Place lobster shells in the centre of four large bowls and fill with warm Basmati Rice. Curl each broiled tail around a sausage and place on top of lobster shell. Carefully spoon gumbo around shell. Garnish with Old Bay Breadsticks.

* Recipe page 132
** Recipe page 129
*** Recipe page 83
**** Recipe page 148

nutrient analysis	Total Energy: 481 calories
	Fat: 8 g
	Saturated Fat: 1 g
per serving	Cholesterol: 83 mg
	Sodium: 511 mg

Stocks, Broths and Sauces

Vegetable Stock

Chicken Stock

Fish Stock

Lobster Broth

Mushroom Broth

Tomato Broth

Corn Broth

Court-Boullion

Yellow Pepper Coulis

Pesto

Chili Black Bean Sauce

Icy Hot Plum Sauce

Honey Mustard Glaze

Soy Ginger Glaze

Simple Syrup

Tomato Coulis

Barbeque Sauce

Chicken Jus

Stocks, Broths and Sauces

Stocks and broths are among the most basic kitchen preparations. They are also an essential component of healthy cooking. Once you understand the basics of making them, you'll be able to vary the ingredients.

You'll soon find that stocks and broths become not only a base for soups and sauces, but also a cooking medium for vegetables and grains, replacing fats and oils.

VEGETABLE STOCK

Makes 4 cups / 1 L

1 teaspoon vegetable oil	5 mL
1 cup roughly chopped onions	250 mL
1 cup roughly chopped celery	250 mL
1 cup roughly chopped carrots	250 mL
1 clove garlic	1
1 bay leaf	1
2 sprigs thyme	2
10 whole peppercorns	10
7 cups cold water	1.7 L

Heat oil in a large stock pot. Sauté onions until soft and add celery, carrots, garlic, bay leaf, thyme, peppercorns and water. Bring to a boil, reduce heat and simmer 45 minutes or until vegetables are soft. Strain and reserve stock.

nutrient analysis per serving

1 cup / 250 mL serving
Total Energy: 49 calories
Fat: 1 g
Saturated Fat: trace
Cholesterol: 0 mg
Sodium: 53 mg

CHICKEN STOCK

Makes 4 cups / 1 L

4 pounds chicken bones	2 kg
2 onions, quartered	2
2 carrots, chopped	2
3 stalks celery, chopped	3
1 clove garlic	1
2 tablespoons tomato paste	25 mL
1/2 cup red wine	125 mL
1 sprig thyme	1
1 bay leaf	1
10 whole peppercorns	10

Seared Chicken Breast with Green Bean "Pecandine" and Stone Fruit Preserve, p.112

Preheat oven to 400 F / 200 C.

In a roasting pan, cook bones in a single layer, being careful not to burn, for 30 minutes or until browned. Stir and add vegetables and tomato paste. Continue roasting until vegetables are browned and tomato paste is lightly caramelized, about 10 minutes. Remove from oven. Place bones and vegetables in a large stock pot. Place roasting pan over high heat and deglaze with red wine. Scrape and remove from heat. Add spices and wine scrapings with enough cold water to cover bones. Bring to a boil and reduce to a slow simmer. Cook 3 to 4 hours or until reduced by one-third, skimming any foam. Strain and refrigerate overnight. Before using, peel away fat that forms on top of the congealed stock.

nutrient analysis per serving	**1 cup / 250 mL serving** **Total Energy: 67 calories** **Fat: trace** **Saturated Fat: trace** **Cholesterol: 0 mg** **Sodium: 47 mg**

FISH STOCK

Makes 4 cups / 1 L

Never cook a fish stock for more than 30 minutes or it may take on an overly fishy aroma and flavour.

1 teaspoon vegetable oil	5 mL
1 small onion, chopped	1
1 leek, chopped	1
1 stalk celery, chopped	1
1 small carrot, chopped	1
1 1/2 pounds lean fish bones, cut in pieces (halibut, haddock, sole, etc.)	750 g
2 sprigs fresh parsley	2
5 cups cold water	1.25 L

Heat oil in a large heavy stock pot and sauté vegetables until soft. Add bones, parsley and water. Bring to a boil then reduce to a simmer. Cook, uncovered, 30 minutes, skimming off any foam. Strain and reserve stock.

nutrient analysis per serving	**Per 1 cup / 250 mL serving** **Total Energy: 42 calories** **Fat: 1 g** **Saturated Fat: trace** **Cholesterol: 0 mg** **Sodium: 30 mg**

Pork Loin with Apple Pistachio Bread Pudding, p.113

LOBSTER BROTH

This lobster-infused broth is the perfect way to impart the flavour of lobster when steaming or poaching fish.

3 cups cold water	750 mL
1/2 cup diced celery	125 mL
1 cup diced onion	250 mL
1/2 cup chopped leeks, green part only	125 mL
3 cloves garlic	3
shells of 2 lobsters, crushed	2
5 black peppercorns	5
1 bay leaf	1
1 cup dry white wine	250 mL

Combine water, celery, onions, leeks, garlic, lobster shells, peppercorns, bay leaf and wine in a large stock pot. Bring to a boil, then lower heat to a simmer. Cook about 30 minutes. Strain and reserve broth.

nutrient analysis

per serving

1 cup / 250 mL serving
Total Energy: 81 calories
Fat: trace
Saturated Fat: trace
Cholesterol: 0 mg
Sodium: 29 mg

MUSHROOM BROTH

Here's a great way to replace chicken stock in vegetarian recipes while maintaining a deep rich flavour and colour.

1 1/2 pounds white button mushrooms, quartered	750 g
1/8 teaspoon kosher salt	0.5 mL
1/8 teaspoon black pepper	0.5 mL
2 shallots, minced	2
2 cloves garlic, halved	2
4 cups Vegetable Stock*	1 L
2 tablespoons minced fresh parsley	25 mL

Heat a large pan, coated with non-stick cooking spray, over medium-high heat. Sauté mushrooms with salt and pepper, stirring constantly, until mushrooms are deep brown in colour and have caramelized, 15 to 20 minutes. Add shallots, garlic and Vegetable Stock. Add parsley and stir well, scraping the pan. Transfer contents to a smaller pot and bring to a boil over medium-high heat. Cook 15 minutes. Remove from heat and strain broth through a fine strainer. The broth will be dark brown in colour.

*Recipe page 128

nutrient analysis per serving	**1 cup / 250 mL serving** **Total Energy: 68 calories** **Fat: 1 g** **Saturated Fat: trace** **Cholesterol: 0 mg** **Sodium: 103 mg**

TOMATO BROTH

Makes 4 cups / 1 L

3 large tomatoes, roughly chopped	*3*
1/2 cup onions, roughly chopped	*125 mL*
1/2 cup celery, roughly chopped	*125 mL*
1/4 cup carrots, roughly chopped	*50 mL*
2 sprigs thyme	*2*
1 clove garlic	*1*
1 tablespoon tomato paste	*15 mL*
1 bay leaf	*1*
5 whole white peppercorns	*5*
1/2 cup dry white wine	*125 mL*
4 cups cold water	*1 L*

Combine tomatoes, onions, celery, carrots, thyme, garlic, tomato paste, bay leaf, peppercorns, wine and water in a large stock pot. Bring to a hard boil, then reduce heat to a slow simmer. Cook 30 minutes. Strain and reserve broth.

nutrient analysis per serving	**1 cup / 250 mL serving** **Total Energy: 60 calories** **Fat: trace** **Saturated Fat: trace** **Cholesterol: 0 mg** **Sodium: 36 mg**

CORN BROTH

4 ears corn, niblets removed	4
1/2 cup diced onion	125 mL
1/4 cup diced celery	50 mL
1/4 cup diced carrot	50 mL
2 cloves garlic	2
pinch of saffron	pinch
1 bay leaf	1
5 white peppercorns	5
5 whole coriander seeds	5
1 cup white wine	250 mL
4 cups cold water	1 L

Combine corn, onions, celery, carrots, garlic, saffron, bay leaf, peppercorns, coriander, wine and water in a large stock pot. Bring to a boil, then reduce heat to a simmer. Cook about 35 minutes. Remove from heat, strain and reserve broth.

nutrient analysis per serving	1 cup / 250 mL serving Total Energy: 218 calories Fat: 2 g Saturated Fat: trace Cholesterol: 0 mg Sodium: 31 mg

COURT-BOUILLON

Court-bouillon is an excellent way to steam or poach saltwater fish and shellfish such as lobster. When working with the more delicate flavours of freshwater fish, replace the water and vinegar with equal parts water and white wine.

4 cups water	1 L
1/4 cup white wine vinegar	50 mL
1 lemon, quartered	1
1 tablespoon kosher salt	15 mL
1 pound mirepoix (chopped onions, leeks, carrots and celery)	500 g
1 teaspoon crushed black peppercorns	5 mL

1 bay leaf	*1*
1/2 bunch fresh parsley	*1/2*

In a large pot over high heat, combine water, vinegar, lemon, salt, mirepoix, peppercorns, bay leaf and parsley. Bring to a boil. Reduce heat to a simmer and cook 45 minutes. Strain and use immediately or cool and refrigerate.

Don't be alarmed at the high sodium content. You are not ingesting this amount when you use this recipe as a medium for steaming or poaching.

nutrient analysis per serving	**1 cup / 250 mL serving** Total Energy: 24 calories Fat: trace Saturated Fat: trace Cholesterol: 0 mg Sodium: 1763 mg

YELLOW PEPPER COULIS

Makes 1/2 cup / 125 mL

This sweet pepper sauce doesn't overpower even the most delicate fish. You won't be disappointed.

1 clove garlic, chopped	*1*
1 tablespoon finely chopped onion	*15 mL*
2 large yellow peppers, chopped	*2*
1/4 cup white wine	*50 mL*
*1 cup Vegetable Stock**	*250 mL*
1/8 teaspoon kosher salt	*0.5 mL*
1/8 teaspoon black pepper	*0.5 mL*

Heat a large pot sprayed with non-stick cooking spray over medium heat. Sauté garlic and onions until translucent without browning. Add peppers and sauté until tender. Deglaze pan with wine. Add Vegetable Stock, bring to a simmer and cook 15 minutes, adding extra stock if necessary. Season with salt and pepper. Purée and strain through a fine sieve.

* Recipe page 128

nutrient analysis per serving	**2 tablespoons / 25 mL serving** Total Energy: 43 calories Fat: trace Saturated Fat: trace Cholesterol: 0 mg Sodium: 81 mg

PESTO

Toss this colourful, flavour-packed paste with hot spaghetti or linguine. The recipe makes enough for six. I also like to toss it with partially-cooked potatoes, then finish roasting them in the oven. Delicious!

1/3 cup basil leaves	75 mL
1/4 cup pine nuts, toasted	50 mL
2 tablespoons extra virgin olive oil	25 mL
1/4 cup freshly grated Parmesan cheese	50 mL
2 cloves garlic, minced	2
Vegetable Stock*	

Combine basil, pine nuts, oil, cheese and garlic in a blender or food processor. Purée to form a coarse paste. While machine is still running, gradually add enough stock to form a smooth paste.

* Recipe page 128

Despite containing almost 10 grams fat per serving, this recipe is still much lower in fat than traditional pesto.

nutrient analysis per serving	2 tablespoons/ 25 mL serving
	Total Energy: 91 calories
	Fat: 9 g
	Saturated Fat: 2 g
	Cholesterol: 3 mg
	Sodium: 63 mg

CHILI BLACK BEAN SAUCE

Makes 1 1/2 cups / 375 mL

This is a great sauce for beef. Everyone will appreciate its warmth and richness.

1 teaspoon Chili Oil*	5 mL
1 small onion, diced	1
1 clove garlic, minced	1
1 jalapeno pepper, seeded and minced	1
1/4 cup diced red pepper	50 mL
1/2 cup white wine	125 mL
1 cup black beans, soaked overnight	250 mL
2 cups Vegetable Stock**	500 mL
2 teaspoons ground cumin	10 mL
1 teaspoon ground coriander seed	5 mL
1/8 teaspoon kosher salt	0.5 mL
1 medium tomato, diced	1
3 sprigs fresh coriander, chopped	3

Heat Chili Oil in a large saucepan over medium heat. Sauté onions, garlic, jalapeno and peppers until tender. Deglaze pan with wine, raise heat and reduce liquid until almost dry. Add black beans, Vegetable Stock, cumin, coriander seed, salt, tomato and fresh coriander. Reduce heat and simmer until beans are tender, about 1 1/2 hours. Remove from heat and transfer two-thirds of the beans to a large bowl. Transfer liquid and remaining beans to a food processor. Purée until smooth, then combine with whole beans. Serve warm, or cover and refrigerate up to 2 days. Thin with extra stock before serving.

* Recipe page 78
**Recipe page 128

nutrient analysis per serving

2 tablespoons / 25 mL serving
Total Energy: 40 calories
Fat: 1 g
Saturated Fat: trace
Cholesterol: 0 mg
Sodium: 36 mg

ICY HOT PLUM SAUCE

Makes 1 cup / 250 mL

This contemporary hot and sour sauce relies on the freshest, ripest red plums for its flavour and colour.

1 teaspoon sesame oil	5 mL
2 pounds ripe plums, halved and pitted	1 kg
1 jalapeno pepper, halved and seeded	1
1 stalk lemongrass	1
2 tablespoons sliced ginger	25 mL ·
1/2 cup granulated sugar	125 mL
1 sprig fresh coriander	1
3 cups rice wine vinegar	750 mL

Heat oil in a large saucepan over medium heat. Add plums, jalapeno, lemongrass and ginger and sauté 5 minutes. Add sugar and coriander and continue cooking 3 minutes. Add vinegar and gently simmer 30 minutes or until liquid has thickened and plums resemble a mushy pulp. Transfer contents of pot to a medium strainer and let stand until all liquid has passed through. Do not push ingredients through strainer as this will result in a cloudy, sometimes bitter sauce.

nutrient analysis

per serving

2 tablespoons / 25 mL serving
Total Energy: 160 calories
Fat: 1 g
Saturated Fat: trace
Cholesterol: 0 mg
Sodium: 12 mg

HONEY MUSTARD GLAZE

Makes 1/2 cup / 125 mL

This sauce is refreshingly simple and works wonderfully with chicken and seafood. Only a small amount is needed to heighten a dish as the flavours are very concentrated.

2 tablespoons Dijon mustard	25 mL
2 tablespoons grainy mustard	25 mL
3 tablespoons rice wine vinegar	45 mL
1 tablespoon honey	15 mL
1 teaspoon Chili Oil*	5 mL

In a large bowl, whisk mustards, vinegar and honey until all ingredients are incorporated. Whisk in Chili Oil. Store, covered, in the refrigerator.

* Recipe page 78

SOY GINGER GLAZE

Makes 1 cup / 250 mL

1/4 cup water	50 mL
juice of 1/2 a lime	1/2
1/4 cup light or low-sodium soy sauce	50 mL
1/2 cup pineapple juice	125 mL
1 tablespoon honey	15 mL
1/2 teaspoon grated ginger	2 mL
1 1/2 teaspoons cornstarch	7 mL

Combine water, lime juice, soy sauce, pineapple juice, honey and ginger in a small saucepan over medium heat. Reduce heat to a simmer and cook 15 minutes. In a small bowl, dissolve cornstarch in 1 1/2 teaspoons/7 mL cold water. When sauce comes to a boil again, whisk in cornstarch mixture. Continue cooking, stirring constantly, until thickened, 3 to 5 minutes. Glaze should be thick enough to coat the back of a spoon. Thin with a little extra pineapple juice if necessary.

SIMPLE SYRUP

Makes 1 cup / 250 mL

Try blending this syrup with fresh mint to make a delicious light sauce for summer fruit.

1 cup granulated sugar	250 mL
1 cup water	250 mL
1/2 cinnamon stick	1/2
1 clove	1

Combine sugar, water, cinnamon and clove in a saucepan over high heat. Bring to a boil and cook until sugar is completely dissolved, about 5 minutes. Remove from heat. Remove cinnamon stick and clove and let cool. Because of its high sugar content, this syrup may begin to crystallize after a few days. Should this occur, simply bring the syrup back to a boil, stirring well.

nutrient analysis

per serving

2 tablespoons/ 25 mL serving
Total Energy: 97 calories
Fat: 0 g
Saturated Fat: 0 g
Cholesterol: 0 mg
Sodium: 1 mg

TOMATO COULIS

Makes 2 cups / 500 mL

A coulis has many functions in gourmet cuisine. The word describes any kind of purée that has been strained to remove solid pieces. This results in a perfectly smooth sauce. A coulis can be used as a sauce, as a flavouring agent for other sauces, or simply to liven up a dish with a splash of colour.

1 teaspoon olive oil	5 mL
1 medium sweet white onion, sliced	1
2 cloves garlic, peeled	2
28-ounce can tomatoes	750 mL
1 bay leaf	1
1 cup Vegetable Stock*	250 mL
1/2 cup red wine	125 mL
2 tablespoons balsamic vinegar	25 mL
1/4 cup chopped fresh herbs (parsley, basil, coriander, etc.)	50 mL
1 teaspoon kosher salt	5 mL
1/2 teaspoon black pepper	2 mL

In a large saucepan, heat oil over medium heat. Sauté onions and garlic until tender. Add tomatoes, bay leaf, Vegetable Stock and wine. Simmer 30 minutes. Remove from heat and transfer tomato mixture to a blender or food processor. Purée until smooth, about 3 minutes. Pass mixture through a coarse strainer and measure volume. If you have more than 2 cups, return to stove and reduce liquid to 2 cups/500 mL. Remove from heat and season with vinegar, herbs, salt and pepper.

* Recipe page 128

nutrient analysis

per serving

2 tablespoons / 25 mL serving
Total Energy: 26 calories
Fat: trace
Saturated Fat: trace
Cholesterol: 0 mg
Sodium: 258 mg

BARBEQUE SAUCE

Makes 1 cup / 250 mL

After making this sauce, you will find it easy to recreate it as your own by adjusting the amount of spice. The best barbeque sauce is always one made from scratch.

3/4 cup ketchup	175 mL
1/3 cup molasses	75 mL
3 tablespoons light or low-sodium soy sauce	45 mL
1 tablespoon dark brown sugar	15 mL
1 teaspoon Dijon mustard	5 mL
1 clove garlic, crushed	1
3 tablespoons lemon juice	45 mL
1/3 cup Chicken Stock*	75 mL
1/4 cup water	50 mL
1 teaspoon Tabasco sauce	5 mL
2 teaspoons Worcestershire sauce	10 mL
1 teaspoon Barbeque Spice Mix**	5 mL
1 jalapeno pepper, seeded	1

Combine all ingredients in a large saucepan and bring to a boil over high heat. Reduce heat to low and simmer 20 minutes. Remove from heat and pass through a fine strainer. Refrigerate in a sealed container up to 5 days.

* Recipe page 128
** Recipe page 144

nutrient analysis

per serving

2 tablespoons / 25 mL serving
Total Energy: 79 calories
Fat: trace
Saturated Fat: trace
Cholesterol: trace
Sodium: 502 mg

CHICKEN JUS

This reduced chicken stock is the foundation for many sauces.

1 teaspoon corn oil	*5 mL*
1 small onion, chopped	*1*
1 clove garlic	*1*
1 bay leaf	*1*
5 black peppercorns	*5*
1/2 bunch parsley stems	*1/2*
2 teaspoons tomato paste	*10 mL*
1/4 cup red wine	*50 mL*
6 cups Chicken Stock*	*1.5 L*

Heat oil in a large saucepan over medium heat. Sauté onions and garlic until translucent and golden, about 5 minutes. Add bay leaf, peppercorns, parsley stems and tomato paste. Cook, stirring constantly, until caramelized, about 5 minutes. Deglaze pan with red wine and reduce until almost dry, about 3 minutes. Add Chicken Stock, reduce heat to a simmer and cook until reduced by two-thirds, about 30 minutes. Remove from heat and pass through a fine strainer or cheesecloth.

* Recipe page 128

nutrient analysis **per serving**	**2 tablespoons/ 25 mL serving** **Total Energy: 97 calories** **Fat: 1 g** **Saturated Fat: trace** **Cholesterol: 0 mg** **Sodium: 57 mg**

Condiments

Barbeque Spice Mix

Old Bay Seasoning

Tortilla Hay

Spiced Pecans

Achiote Marinade

Old Bay Breadsticks

Citrus Corn Crackers

Caramelized Onion Pear Dip

"Red Hot" Red Onions

Tomato Ketchup

Chili Tomato Jam

Homemade Steak Sauce

Southern Corn Chow-Chow

Mango Salsa

Pineapple Relish

Roasted Pepper Salsa

Stone Fruit Preserve

Apple Cranberry Compote

Sundried Cherry Compote

Green Curry

Condiments

The real advantage to making your own condiments is that, with few exceptions, they taste better and have a significantly lower sodium content than storebought varieties.

BARBEQUE SPICE MIX

Makes 1/3 cup / 75 mL

This spice mix is a staple in our kitchen. We find that it complements almost everything, from Spiced Pecans to Chili-Charred Flank Steak.

2 tablespoons paprika	25 mL
1 tablespoon chili powder	15 mL
1 teaspoon ground cumin	5 mL
1 teaspoon ground coriander	5 mL
1 teaspoon granulated sugar	5 mL
1 teaspoon salt	5 mL
1/2 teaspoon dry mustard	2 mL
1/2 teaspoon black pepper	2 mL
1/2 teaspoon dried oregano	2 mL
1/2 teaspoon cayenne pepper	2 mL

Mix all ingredients and store in a cool dry place.

nutrient analysis

per serving

1 teaspoon/5 mL
Total Energy: 7 calories
Fat: trace
Saturated Fat: 0 g
Cholesterol: 0 mg
Sodium: 157 mg

OLD BAY SEASONING

Makes 1/3 cup / 75 mL

Make this aromatic mixture in small amounts and use up before the fragrance fades.

2 tablespoons mustard seeds	*25 mL*
1 tablespoon black peppercorns	*15 mL*
1 tablespoon chili flakes	*15 mL*
3 bay leaves	*3*
1 1/2 teaspoons celery seeds	*7 mL*
1 1/2 teaspoons coriander seed	*7 mL*
1 1/2 teaspoons ground ginger	*7 mL*
1/8 teaspoon ground mace	*0.5 mL*
1 tablespoon salt	*15 mL*

Combine mustard seeds, peppercorns, chili flakes, bay leaves, celery seeds, coriander seeds, ginger and mace in a food processor. Blend until evenly ground.
Add salt and blend briefly to incorporate.
Store, covered, in a cool dry place.

nutrient analysis per serving

1 teaspoon/5 mL
Total Energy: 11 calories
Fat: 0.5 g
Saturated Fat: trace
Cholesterol: 0 mg
Sodium: 437 mg

TORTILLA HAY

Makes 2 cups / 500 mL

8 raw corn tortillas, julienned	*8*

Preheat oven to 250 F / 120 C.
Lightly spray tortilla strips with non-stick cooking spray. Scatter strips evenly on cookie sheet and bake until crisp, 4 to 5 minutes.

nutrient analysis per serving

1/4 cup/50 mL
Total Energy: 55 calories
Fat: trace
Saturated Fat: trace
Cholesterol: 0 mg
Sodium: 40 mg

SPICED PECANS

Makes 3 cups / 750 mL

Don't get carried away while snacking, which is easy to do with this delicious recipe.

2 tablespoons margarine	*25 mL*
3 cups pecan halves	*750 mL*
1/2 cup brown sugar	*125 mL*
2 tablespoons Barbeque Spice Mix*	*25 mL*
1/4 cup cider vinegar	*50 mL*

Preheat oven to 300 F / 150 C.
In a large skillet, melt margarine over medium heat. Add pecans and sauté until lightly browned. Add sugar and cook until caramelized. Stir in the Barbeque Spice Mix. Deglaze pan with vinegar and reduce until dry. Spread pecans on a parchment-lined cookie sheet and bake until crisp, about 5 minutes.

The fat in pecans is mostly monounsaturated and polyunsaturated – both heart-healthy fat choices. Go easy with the amount, however, because all fats are very calorie dense.

* Recipe page 144

nutrient analysis per serving	1/4 cup/50 mL
	Total Energy: 247 calories
	Fat: 22 g
	Saturated Fat: 2 g
	Cholesterol: 0 mg
	Sodium: 173 mg

ACHIOTE MARINADE

Makes 1 cup / 250 mL

The brilliant rusty red of achiote seeds gives food the essence of spice without the heat. Achiote is sometimes called the "saffron" of Mexico because its earthy aroma is valued as much as the flavour of saffron. In this marinade, which is excellent with seafood, it provides flavour and colour.

2 tablespoons achiote powder	25 mL
1/4 cup corn oil	50 mL
1/2 cup chopped onion	125 mL
2 chipotle peppers	2
1 tablespoon black pepper	15 mL
3 tablespoons chopped fresh coriander	45 mL
1 teaspoon lime juice	5 mL

Combine all ingredients in a food processor. Blend until smooth.

nutrient analysis

per serving

1 teaspoon/5 mL
Total Energy: 11 calories
Fat: 1 g
Saturated Fat: trace
Cholesterol: 0 mg
Sodium: 3 mg

OLD BAY BREADSTICKS

Makes 24 thin breadsticks

If you don't have time to make Old Bay Seasoning, buy a commercial brand.

1 3/4 teaspoons active dry yeast	*9 mL*
1 tablespoon malt syrup or molasses	*15 mL*
1 1/4 cups warm water	*300 mL*
2 tablespoons corn oil, plus some for brushing dough	*25 mL*
3 3/4 cups all-purpose flour	*925 mL*
1 tablespoon Old Bay Seasoning*	*15 mL*
1 1/2 teaspoons salt	*7 mL*
1/2 cup cornmeal	*125 mL*

Stir yeast and malt syrup into warm water in large bowl of an electric mixer. Let stand until foamy, about 10 minutes. Mix in oil on low speed. Add flour, Old Bay and salt. Mix until dough comes together in a ball. Change to dough hook attachment and knead at low speed 3 minutes. Finish kneading briefly by hand on a lightly-floured surface.

Pat dough with your hands into a 14x4-inch / 35x10cm rectangle on a well-floured surface. Lightly brush top with oil. Cover with plastic wrap and let rise until doubled, about 1 hour.

Preheat oven to 450 F / 230 C.

Sprinkle dough with cornmeal before cutting and shaping. Cut dough into thin strips about 1/4-inch/0.5cm thick and place on a parchment-lined cookie sheet 1-inch/2.5 cm apart. Bake 10 to 12 minutes, or until lightly golden. Cool on wire racks.

* Recipe page 145

nutrient analysis per serving	**1 breadstick** **Total Energy: 91 calories** **Fat: 1 g** **Saturated Fat: trace** **Cholesterol: 0 mg** **Sodium: 221 mg**

CITRUS CORN CRACKERS

Makes 24 crackers

Here is one of the easiest forms of flatbread to make. Since it doesn't require yeast, this recipe can be prepared in little or no time at all.

1/4 cup cornmeal	*50 mL*
1/4 cup all-purpose flour	*50 mL*
1/8 teaspoon salt	*0.5 mL*
1 teaspoon finely chopped orange zest	*5 mL*
cayenne pepper to taste	
1 tablespoon finely chopped fresh thyme	*15 mL*
1 tablespoon lemon juice	*15 mL*
1/2 cup orange juice or as needed	*125 mL*

Preheat oven to 300 F / 150 C.
Blend cornmeal in food processor until it resembles fine dust. Add flour, salt, orange zest, cayenne and thyme. Process until thoroughly combined. Add lemon juice and slowly add enough orange juice to form a spreadable paste. Spread batter thinly onto parchment-lined cookie sheets and bake until crispy, about 6 minutes. Cool completely and break into bite-sized pieces.

nutrient analysis

per serving

1 cracker
Total Energy: 12 calories
Fat: 0 g
Saturated Fat: 0 g
Cholesterol: 0 mg
Sodium: 13 mg

CARAMELIZED ONION PEAR DIP

Makes 1 cup/250 mL

Onions and pears combine to make the perfect autumn condiment. We serve it with grilled beef skewers.

1 medium onion, sliced	*1*
3 small ripe pears, peeled and chopped	*3*
1 tablespoon apple cider	*15 mL*
1/4 cup cider vinegar	*50 mL*
1 Spice Bag:	
1/2 cinnamon stick	
3 cloves	
1 star anise	

In a large saucepan sprayed with non-stick cooking spray, sauté onions over medium heat until brown and caramelized but not burnt, about 10 minutes. Add remaining ingredients and reduce heat to low. Cook mixture until almost dry, being careful not to burn, about 30 minutes. Remove spice bag and transfer to a food processor or blender. Blend until smooth. Serve at room temperature.

nutrient analysis

per serving

2 tablespoons/25 mL
Total Energy: 49 calories
Fat: trace
Saturated Fat: trace
Cholesterol: 0 mg
Sodium: 1 mg

"RED HOT" RED ONIONS

Makes 2 cups/500mL

I use these fiery pickled onions on everything. If you like things hot, I'm sure you'll find yourself doing the same.

3 medium red onions, thinly sliced	3
1 teaspoon salt	5 mL
2 cups raspberry vinegar	500 mL
1 small beet, peeled and diced	1
2 jalapeno peppers, split in half	2
1 bay leaf	1
5 coriander seeds	5
5 black peppercorns	5
1/2 cinnamon stick	1/2
2 teaspoons granulated sugar	10 mL

Place onions in a sterilized, swing-top Mason jar.

Combine remaining ingredients in a medium saucepan. Bring to a boil. Reduce heat to a gentle simmer and cook until bright red, about 10 minutes. Strain liquid into a container and cool completely. Pour liquid over the sliced onions and seal jar.

Refrigerate at least overnight before using, to blend flavours.

nutrient analysis

per serving

1 tablespoon / 15 mL
Total Energy: 10 calories
Fat: trace
Saturated Fat: 0 g
Cholesterol: 0 mg
Sodium: 77 mg

TOMATO KETCHUP

Makes 1 cup / 250 mL

Although there are many bottled versions around that are tasty and convenient, when this ketchup is made with the freshest tomatoes you can really taste the difference.

2 pounds very ripe tomatoes, cored and chopped	1 kg
1 large onion, chopped	1
8 sundried tomatoes	8
1/3 cup cider vinegar	75 mL
1/4 cup brown sugar	50 mL
1 cinnamon stick	1
1/4 teaspoon cayenne powder	1 mL
1/4 teaspoon ground cloves	1 mL
pinch of mace	pinch
1/8 teaspoon kosher salt	0.5 mL

In a large saucepan over medium heat, simmer tomatoes and onions until pulpy, about 30 minutes. Remove from heat and push the pulp through a sieve to remove seeds and skin. Return pulp to pot and add remaining ingredients. Bring to a simmer. Cook 1 1/2 to 2 hours or until thickened to the consistency of bottled ketchup. Remove from heat and discard cinnamon stick. Transfer ingredients to a food processor and purée mixture until smooth. Let cool. Refrigerate, covered, for several weeks.

nutrient analysis

per serving

1 tablespoon/15 mL
Total Energy: 32 calories
Fat: trace
Saturated Fat: 0 g
Cholesterol: 0 mg
Sodium: 56 mg

CHILI TOMATO JAM

Makes 1 cup / 250 mL

Brown sugar and cider vinegar bring out the taste of tomatoes. I like to use this as a sweet and sour spread on sandwiches.

2x28-ounce cans tomatoes, with juice	*1.5 L*
1 large onion, chopped	*1*
1/2 cup apple cider or juice	*125 mL*
1/4 cup cider vinegar	*50 mL*
1 chipotle pepper	*1*
3 tablespoons brown sugar	*45 mL*
1/4 cup root beer	*50 mL*
Spice Bag :	
1/2 cinnamon stick	
1 clove	
5 coriander seeds	
1 star anise	

In a large stock pot over high heat, combine all ingredients. Bring to a boil, then lower heat to a simmer. Cook 2 hours or until mixture is very thick and almost dry. Stir often to avoid sticking and burning.

nutrient analysis

per serving

1 tablespoon/15 mL
Total Energy: 42 calories
Fat: trace
Saturated Fat: 0 g
Cholesterol: 0 mg
Sodium: 0 mg

HOMEMADE STEAK SAUCE

Makes 1 cup / 250 mL

Every great steak deserves this homemade steak sauce. Try it once and you'll understand why.

1 tablespoon tamarind paste	15 mL
2 tablespoons brown sugar	25 mL
1 cup ketchup	250 mL
1/2 cup light or low-sodium soy sauce	125 mL
1 tablespoon Barbeque Spice Mix*	15 mL
1/4 cup rice vinegar	50 mL
3/4 cup Chicken Stock**	175 mL
1 teaspoon minced ginger	5 mL
1 clove garlic, minced	1
1/2 teaspoon black pepper	2 mL

Combine all ingredients in a saucepan and simmer over medium heat until sauce coats the back of a spoon, about 30 minutes. Transfer to a food processor and blend until smooth. Strain and serve. Refrigerate any remaining sauce in a tightly covered jar up to 1 week.

* Recipe page 144
** Recipe page 128

This sauce is at the high end of sodium per serving. Use it as your one salty item for the day.

nutrient analysis	2 tablespoons/25 mL
	Total Energy: 71 calories
	Fat: trace
per serving	Saturated Fat: trace
	Cholesterol: 0 mg
	Sodium: 1069 mg

SOUTHERN CORN CHOW-CHOW

Makes 2 cups / 500 mL

This corn relish embodies the taste of summer. It's really worth making when corn is in peak season.

1 cup corn niblets (2 small ears)	250 mL
1 tablespoon diced onion	15 mL
1/2 cup diced celery	125 mL
1/4 cup diced yellow pepper	50 mL
1 cup diced cabbage	250 mL
1/2 cup granulated sugar	125 mL
1 1/2 teaspoons all-purpose flour	7 mL
1/4 teaspoon dry mustard	1 mL
1/4 teaspoon turmeric	1 mL
1 teaspoon celery seeds	5 mL
1 teaspoon salt	5 mL
1 cup white vinegar	250 mL

Spray a large saucepan with non-stick cooking spray and place over medium heat. Gently sauté corn, onions, celery, peppers, cabbage, sugar, flour, mustard, turmeric, celery seeds and salt until tender, about 8 minutes. Add vinegar and simmer, stirring constantly until fully cooked, about 10 minutes. Remove from heat, pour into sterilized jars and refrigerate.

nutrient analysis

per serving

2 tablespoons/25 mL
Total Energy: 46 calories
Fat: trace
Saturated Fat: 0 g
Cholesterol: 0 mg
Sodium: 42 mg

MANGO SALSA

Makes 1 cup / 250 mL

Mangoes, India's national fruit, have been grown for over 4,000 years. They range in size from a small peach to a four-pound giant. With their array of colours, shapes and flavours, mangoes are now considered one of the most important tropical fruits.

1/2 cup ripe mango, peeled and finely diced	125 mL
1/4 cup chopped fresh chives	50 mL
1/4 cup red pepper, finely diced	50 mL
1 tablespoon chopped fresh coriander	15 mL
1 tablespoon lemon juice	15 mL
1 jalapeno pepper, seeded and minced	1
Black pepper to taste	
1 teaspoon Chili Oil*	5 mL

Combine all ingredients in a small stainless steel bowl. Cover with plastic wrap and let stand at least 1 hour before serving to blend flavours.

* Recipe page 78

nutrient analysis

per serving

1 tablespoon/15 mL
Total Energy: 9 calories
Fat: trace
Saturated Fat: trace
Cholesterol: 0 mg
Sodium: 5 mg

PINEAPPLE RELISH

Makes 2 cups / 500 mL

Once you know how to combine fruit with a savoury mixture, a world of relish possibilities opens. Use this recipe as a starting point.

1/2 red pepper, finely chopped	1/2
1 jalapeno pepper, seeded and finely chopped	1
1 small red onion, finely diced	1
1 poblano or Anaheim chili, seeded and finely chopped	1
1/2 cup finely diced fresh pineapple	125 mL
1/2 cup finely diced papaya	125 mL
1/2 cup finely diced mango	125 mL
juice of 2 limes	2
3 tablespoons chopped fresh coriander	45 mL
1/8 teaspoon black pepper	0.5 mL

In a large bowl, combine all ingredients. Let stand at room temperature at least 1 hour before serving.

nutrient analysis

per serving

2 tablespoons/25 mL
Total Energy: 13 calories
Fat: trace
Saturated Fat: 0 g
Cholesterol: 0 mg
Sodium: 14 mg

ROASTED PEPPER SALSA

This great multi-purpose salsa goes well with most grilled poultry and fish.

1 cup diced roasted red pepper	250 mL
1/4 cup diced roasted yellow pepper	50 mL
1/4 cup diced red onion	50 mL
1 ear corn, lightly grilled and niblets removed	1
1/4 cup diced poblano chili	50 mL
1 teaspoon jalapeno pepper, seeded and minced	5 mL
2 tablespoons chopped fresh coriander	25 mL
1 tablespoon lemon juice	15 mL
1 teaspoon corn oil	5 mL
1/8 teaspoon kosher salt	0.5 mL
1/2 teaspoon black pepper	2 mL

Combine all ingredients in a medium stainless steel bowl. Toss until well mixed. Let stand at room temperature at least 1 hour before serving to blend flavours.

nutrient analysis

per serving

2 tablespoons/25 mL
Total Energy: 18 calories
Fat: trace
Saturated Fat: trace
Cholesterol: 0 mg
Sodium: 83 mg

STONE FRUIT PRESERVE

Makes 1 cup / 250 mL

Savoury fruit sauces have long been popular in Canada as an accompaniment to many types of meat. Everyone is familiar with mint jelly and cranberry sauce. Now try our zesty version.

1/4 cup dried apricots, quartered	50 mL
1/4 cup diced peaches	50 mL
1/4 cup diced nectarines	50 mL
1/4 cup diced plums	50 mL
1/2 cup apple cider	125 mL
1/2 cup cider vinegar	125 mL
1/4 cup granulated sugar	50 mL
2 cloves	2
1/2 cinnamon stick	1/2
1 1/2 tablespoons cornstarch, dissolved in 1 1/2 tablespoons water	22 mL

Combine apricots, peaches, nectarines, plums, cider, vinegar, sugar, cloves and cinnamon in a saucepan. Simmer over medium heat until fruit is soft and completely cooked, about 5 minutes. Strain liquid into a small pot and return to heat. Reserve fruit. Bring liquid to a boil and slowly whisk in cornstarch until sauce coats the back of a metal spoon. Boil about 1 minute to cook out the starch. Remove from heat, remove cinnamon stick and cloves and combine liquid with the fruit. Serve warm or cold.

nutrient analysis per serving

2 tablespoons/25 mL
Total Energy: 55 calories
Fat: trace
Saturated Fat: 0 g
Cholesterol: 0 mg
Sodium: 1 mg

APPLE CRANBERRY COMPOTE

Makes 3 cups/ 750 mL

Use this compote instead of traditional cranberry sauce for your next Thanksgiving dinner. Share it with friends and family by sealing any extra in a Mason jar.

1 cup granulated sugar	250 mL
1/2 cup white wine vinegar	125 mL
2 medium Granny Smith apples, peeled and diced	2
1 shallot, minced	1
zest of 1 lemon, finely chopped	1
juice of 1 lemon	1
1/8 teaspoon ground cinnamon	0.5 mL
1/4 teaspoon whole mustard seed	1 mL
2 cloves	2
1/2 teaspoon kosher salt	2 mL
1 cup fresh or thawed cranberries	250 mL

In a stainless steel saucepan, combine sugar, vinegar, apples and shallots. Add lemon zest and juice, spices and salt. Place saucepan over medium heat and bring to a simmer. Lower heat and simmer 10 minutes, stirring every few minutes. Add cranberries and simmer until almost dry, 8 to 10 minutes. Remove from heat, cool and refrigerate.

nutrient analysis

per serving

2 tablespoons/25 mL
Total Energy: 42 calories
Fat: 0 g
Saturated Fat: 0 g
Cholesterol: 0 mg
Sodium: 47 mg

Tandoori-Roasted Swordfish with Pineapple Relish and Green Cardamom Basmati, p. 117

SUNDRIED CHERRY COMPOTE

Makes 1 cup/ 250 mL

The tartness of dried cherries makes a classic marriage with pork and game.

1 cup sundried cherries	*250 mL*
1 cup apple cider	*250 mL*
1/4 cup cider vinegar	*50 mL*
2 tablespoons brown sugar	*25 mL*
1/8 teaspoon kosher salt	*0.5 mL*
1/4 teaspoon ground allspice	*1 mL*
1/4 teaspoon ground cinnamon	*1 mL*
1/8 teaspoon ground cloves	*0.5 mL*
1/8 teaspoon ground nutmeg	*0.5 mL*
cayenne pepper to taste	

In a medium saucepan over high heat, bring all ingredients to a boil. Cook about 7 minutes, or until liquid is reduced by half. Reduce heat to a simmer and cook 10 minutes or until cherries have rehydrated and liquid is thickened. Remove from heat, transfer compote to a container. Let cool. Store in a covered jar in the refrigerator.

nutrient analysis

per serving

2 tablespoons/25 mL
Total Energy: 128 calories
Fat: 1 g
Saturated Fat: 0 g
Cholesterol: 0 mg
Sodium: 45 mg

Grilled Atlantic Salmon on Black and Gold Pasta with Japanese Miso and Green Onion Sauce, p.123

GREEN CURRY

To avoid the saturated fat in canned coconut milk while preserving the flavour, let the can sit, undisturbed, in the refrigerator overnight. The milk solids will separate from the water. When opening the can, be careful not to shake it too much.

1 jalapeno pepper, seeded	1
1 bunch fresh coriander, chopped	1
3 green onions, green only, chopped	3
1/4 cup curry powder	50 mL
2 tablespoons ground cumin	25 mL
3 tablespoons rice wine vinegar	45 mL
1 teaspoon minced garlic	5 mL
1/2 cup coconut water	125 mL

Combine all ingredients in a blender or food processor and blend until smooth. Pass through a medium sieve.

nutrient analysis per serving

1 tablespoon/15 mL
Total Energy: 9 calories
Fat: trace
Saturated Fat: 0 g
Cholesterol: 0 mg
Sodium: 37 mg

Desserts and Cookies

Sugar Cookies

Chocolate Orange Cookies

Sundried Cherry Biscotti

Espresso Granita Float

Ginger Crème Brûlée

Cherry Clafouti

Apple Plum Crisp

Lemon Pudding Cake

Carrot Cake

Chewy Chocolate Brownies

Chocolate Cake with Cocoa Frosting

Mango Sorbet with Blueberry Compote

Toasted Angel Food Cake with Pumpkin Chiffon

Desserts and Cookies

For me, dinner is incomplete without dessert. Whether it's a plate of cookies or a chocolate layer cake, dessert sends the message: "Sit back, relax, and enjoy something sweet."

All the recipes in this chapter are easy to make, so you won't have to choose between making the meal and making dessert. And who would imagine that our Chewy Chocolate Brownies could taste so good, and yet contain only five grams of fat per serving?

SUGAR COOKIES

Makes 24 cookies

1/4 cup margarine, softened	50 mL
1/2 cup granulated sugar	125 mL
2 tablespoons egg substitute	25 mL
1 tablespoon skim milk	15 mL
1/2 teaspoon vanilla extract	2 mL
1 cup all-purpose flour	250 mL
1 teaspoon baking powder	5 mL
1/4 teaspoon salt	1 mL
pinch of nutmeg	pinch

Preheat oven to 375 F / 190 C.
In a medium bowl, cream together margarine and sugar. Beat in egg substitute, milk and vanilla until fluffy. In a separate bowl, sift together flour, baking powder, salt and nutmeg. Combine with egg mixture and beat until smooth. Refrigerate until well chilled. Lightly coat a cookie sheet with non-stick cooking spray. Form dough into balls 1-inch/2.5 cm in diameter and arrange on tray. Lightly press your thumb into centre of each cookie. Bake 8 minutes. Cool on a rack.

nutrient analysis

per serving

1 cookie
Total Energy: 52 calories
Fat: 2 g
Saturated Fat: trace
Cholesterol: 0 mg
Sodium: 69 mg

CHOCOLATE ORANGE COOKIES

Makes 40 cookies

1 cup all-purpose flour	250 mL
1/2 cup plus 1 tablespoon cocoa powder	125 mL + 15 mL
1/4 teaspoon baking powder	1 mL
2 teaspoons finely chopped orange zest	10 mL
pinch of cinnamon	pinch
1 teaspoon salt	5 mL
1/2 cup plus 1 tablespoon brown sugar	125 mL + 15 mL
1/2 cup plus 1 tablespoon granulated sugar	125 mL + 15 mL
3 tablespoons unsalted butter	45 mL
3 tablespoons margarine	45 mL
1 teaspoon Grand Marnier or other orange liqueur	5 mL
1 egg white	1

Preheat oven to 350 F / 180 C.

Combine flour, cocoa, baking powder, orange zest, cinnamon and salt in a medium bowl. Mix thoroughly with a whisk. Combine sugars in a separate bowl, pressing out any lumps with your fingers. Set aside.

With an electric mixer, beat butter and margarine until creamy. Add sugars and Grand Marnier. Beat on high speed about 1 minute. Beat in egg white. On low speed, beat in flour mixture until just incorporated. Gather dough with your hands and form into a neat 10-inch/25cm log. Wrap with parchment and chill 1 hour. Using a sharp knife, slice log into 1/4-inch/0.5cm rounds and arrange on a parchment-lined cookie sheet. Bake 12 to 14 minutes, rotating often for even baking.

nutrient analysis per serving	1 cookie
	Total Energy: 64 calories
	Fat: 3 g
	Saturated Fat: 1 g
	Cholesterol: 3 mg
	Sodium: 78 mg

SUNDRIED CHERRY BISCOTTI

Makes about 20 cookies

Crunchy biscotti are traditionally dipped in Italy's sweet Vin Santo wine after dinner.

1 cup all-purpose flour	*250 mL*
1/2 cup granulated sugar	*125 mL*
1/4 teaspoon salt	*1 mL*
1/2 teaspoon baking powder	*2 mL*
1 teaspoon each finely chopped lemon and orange zest	*10 mL*
1 egg	*1*
1 egg yolk	*1*
1/2 teaspoon vanilla extract	*2 mL*
3/4 cup sundried cherries	*175 mL*

Preheat oven to 325 F / 170 C.

Place flour, sugar, salt, baking powder and fruit zest in bowl of an electric mixer. Combine on medium-low speed. In a separate bowl, lightly whisk together egg, egg yolk and vanilla. Pour egg mixture into dry ingredients while continuing to mix. When egg is almost incorporated, add cherries and reduce speed to low. Continue to mix until dough comes together.

Roll dough into a 10x2-inch/25x5 cm log. Place log on a parchment-lined cookie sheet and bake until light brown, about 20 minutes. Remove from oven and let cool. Reduce oven temperature to 300 F/150 C. Cut log at a slight diagonal, 1/2-inch/1 cm thick. Return biscotti to cookie sheet, cut-side up. Bake 15 minutes longer or until golden brown and dry.

nutrient analysis per serving	1 cookie
	Total Energy: 74 calories
	Fat: 1 g
	Saturated Fat: trace
	Cholesterol: 21 mg
	Sodium: 42 mg

ESPRESSO GRANITA FLOAT

Serves 12

A refreshing ice made without an ice cream machine, granita supplies the perfect ending to a wonderful summer meal.

Granita:

8 cups chilled espresso coffee	2 L
3 cups granulated sugar	750 mL

Pour espresso into a large bowl. Stir in sugar. Pour sweetened espresso into a shallow 9x13-inch/22x32 cm pan and place in the freezer. Every half hour, roughly stir up the freezing mixture with a whisk or a fork. This will give the granita its icy texture. Freeze espresso overnight or until completely frozen.

Espresso Yogurt:

1 cup non-fat cottage cheese	250 mL
2 cups non-fat plain yogurt	500 mL
1 cup granulated sugar	250 mL
1/4 cup brewed espresso coffee	50 mL
2 teaspoons vanilla extract	10 mL

In a blender, process cottage cheese until smooth. Transfer to a large bowl and combine with yogurt and sugar. Mix well. Add espresso and vanilla and mix until smooth.
Spoon granita into 12 champagne flutes or other tall narrow glasses. Spoon espresso yogurt on top. Serve immediately.

nutrient analysis per serving	Total Energy: 296 calories
	Fat: trace
	Saturated Fat: trace
	Cholesterol: 2 mg
	Sodium: 107 mg

GINGER CREME BRULEE

This low-fat version of the traditional custard is combined with the same spices as gingerbread, creating an excellent finish to a holiday meal.

1/3 cup granulated sugar	75 mL
2 tablespoons cornstarch	25 mL
1/8 teaspoon salt	0.5 mL
pinch each of nutmeg, cinnamon and cloves	pinch
1 teaspoon ground ginger	5 mL
2 cups evaporated skim milk	500 mL
1/2 cup egg substitute	125 mL
2 egg whites	2
1 1/2 teaspoons vanilla extract	7 mL
4 teaspoons granulated sugar	20 mL

Combine sugar, cornstarch, salt, nutmeg, cinnamon, cloves and ginger in a small bowl. Add just enough evaporated milk to create a smooth paste. Set aside. Bring remaining milk to a boil in a 2-quart/2 L saucepan.

Meanwhile, in a medium bowl, whisk together egg substitute, egg whites and vanilla. Gradually whisk one-third of the boiling milk into sugar mixture and return to saucepan. Bring to a gentle simmer and cook, stirring, about 2 minutes. Remove milk from heat and gradually whisk 1 cup/250 mL into the eggs to prevent scrambling. Pour egg mixture into saucepan. Cook, without allowing to boil or simmer, for 2 minutes while stirring constantly. Pour immediately into 4 individual ramekins. Chill at least 4 hours.

Preheat oven broiler.

Lightly sprinkle tops of each custard with 1 teaspoon/5 mL sugar. Caramelize under broiler until brown and bubbly, about 2 minutes.

nutrient analysis

per serving

Total Energy: 235 calories
Fat: 1 g
Saturated Fat: trace
Cholesterol: 5 mg
Sodium: 298 mg

CHERRY CLAFOUTI

This classic French dessert is easy to prepare and delightful to serve.

1 1/2 pounds fresh cherries, pitted	750 g
1 1/4 cups skim milk	300 mL
1/4 cup firmly packed brown sugar	50 mL
1/4 teaspoon cinnamon	1 mL
3 eggs	3
1 tablespoon vanilla extract	15 mL
1 teaspoon almond extract	5 mL
1 cup all-purpose flour	250 mL
1/4 teaspoon ground mace	1 mL
1/4 teaspoon salt	1 mL
3 tablespoons slivered almonds	45 mL
1 tablespoon granulated sugar	15 mL

Preheat oven to 350 F / 180 C.

Lightly spray a 9-inch/22 cm pie plate or 8 individual ramekins with non-stick cooking spray. Set aside.

In a food processor, combine milk, brown sugar, cinnamon, eggs, extracts, flour, mace and salt. Process until mixture forms a smooth batter. Pour about 1 cup /250 mL batter into pie plate or pour 2 tablespoons/25 mL batter into each ramekin.

Bake 5 minutes or until set.

Remove pan from oven and evenly distribute cherries on top of cooked batter. Pour remaining batter over top. Bake 20 to 25 minutes, then sprinkle almonds and sugar over top. Bake 30 minutes more. Serve warm.

nutrient analysis	Total Energy: 224 calories
	Fat: 5 g
	Saturated Fat: 1 g
per serving	Cholesterol: 80 mg
	Sodium: 119 mg

APPLE PLUM CRISP

Serves 10

There is more behind the idea of a crisp than just flavour. Early North American cooks usually made between 5 and 10 pies at a time. But the bottom crust would go soggy unless the pie was eaten the day it was baked. A crumbly topping solved this problem, remaining "crisp" for days without requiring a bottom crust.

3 pounds apples	1.5 kg
1 pound ripe plums, pitted and sliced	500 g
1/3 cup brown sugar	75 mL
1 1/2 tablespoons all-purpose flour, plus 2 tablespoons	22 mL + 25 mL
juice of 1 orange	1
1/2 teaspoon ground cinnamon	2 mL
1 cup rolled oats	250 mL
1/4 cup unsalted butter or margarine	50 mL
zest of 1 orange	1

Preheat oven to 450 F / 220 C and adjust shelf to top third of oven.

Wash, peel and core apples. Slice about 1/4-inch/0.5 cm thick. Place in a large bowl with plums, 1 tablespoon/15 mL brown sugar, flour, orange juice and cinnamon.

Spread fruit mixture in an 8x14-inch/20x35 cm glass baking dish.

Blend oats, butter, orange zest and remaining brown sugar by hand until well mixed. Spread oat mixture over fruit and bake 25 to 35 minutes. If topping begins to burn, cover dish loosely with aluminum foil. Serve warm.

nutrient analysis per serving	Total Energy: 206 calories Fat: 6 g Saturated Fat: 1 g Cholesterol: 0 mg Sodium: 65 mg

LEMON PUDDING CAKE

Serves 10

This refreshing cake has an intense lemon flavour.

2/3 cup granulated sugar	150 mL
1 1/2 cups skim milk	375 mL
1/2 cup all-purpose flour	125 mL
1/8 teaspoon salt	0.5 mL
2 tablespoons margarine, melted	25 mL
1 tablespoon grated lemon rind	15 mL
1/3 cup lemon juice	75 mL
1 teaspoon vanilla extract	5 mL
3 eggs, separated	3
1 tablespoon granulated sugar	15 mL

Preheat oven to 350 F / 180 C.

Lightly spray an 8-inch/20cm square baking pan with non-stick cooking spray.

In a large mixing bowl, combine sugar, milk, flour, salt, margarine, lemon rind and juice, vanilla and egg yolks. Beat until smooth. Set aside.

In a small mixing bowl, beat egg whites until soft peaks form. Add remaining sugar and beat until stiff. Mix one-third of whites into lemon mixture. Fold in remaining whites.

Pour batter into prepared pan. Bake in a water bath 45 to 50 minutes. Serve warm.

* A water bath increases the moisture content in the oven to keep baked goods moist. In a large shallow baking pan, pour 1/2-inch/1cm of warm water. Place in the oven, then carefully set the filled cake pan in it. Bake as directed.

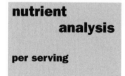

nutrient analysis

per serving

Total Energy: 135 calories
Fat: 4 g
Saturated Fat: 1 g
Cholesterol: 64 mg
Sodium: 98 mg

"Red Hot" Red Onions, p.151 Southern Corn Chow-Chow, p.155

CARROT CAKE

David let me sneak in this recipe because it's a perfect example of how applesauce can replace oil or margarine in cake and quickbread recipes. The original recipe called for 1 1/4 cups/300 mL oil. Colleague, Maria D'Agrosa, RD and I played around with several variations until we came up with this one.

2 cups granulated sugar	500 mL
1 cup unsweetened applesauce	250 mL
1/4 cup canola oil	50 mL
4 eggs	4
2 cups all-purpose flour	500 mL
1 1/2 teaspoons cinnamon	7 mL
1/2 teaspoon nutmeg	2 mL
1 teaspoon salt	5 mL
2 teaspoons baking soda	10 mL
1 cup dark raisins	250 mL
3 1/2 cups grated carrot	875 mL
Cream Cheese Frosting:	
2 cups icing sugar	500 mL
4 ounces light cream cheese	125 g
1 tablespoon skim milk	15 mL
1 teaspoon vanilla extract	5 mL

Preheat oven to 375 F / 190 C.
Spray a tube or bundt pan with non-stick cooking spray.
In a large bowl, combine sugar, applesauce and oil. Mix until smooth. Add eggs one at a time until smooth and fluffy. Sift together flour, cinnamon, nutmeg, salt and baking soda. Combine flour mixture with sugar mixture and blend until smooth. Fold in raisins and carrots. Pour mixture into prepared pan and bake until a cake tester comes out clean, 50 to 60 minutes. Remove from heat and let cool.
In a large mixing bowl, blend icing sugar, cream cheese, milk and vanilla until smooth. Turn cake out of pan. When cool, frost with Cream Cheese Frosting.

The original recipe contained 20 grams of fat per serving. Now, at only 6 grams fat per serving, the flavour and texture are unbeatable.

nutrient analysis	**Total Energy: 316 calories**
	Fat: 6 g
	Saturated Fat: 1 g
per serving	**Cholesterol: 56 mg**
	Sodium: 359 mg

Apple Plum Crisp, p.171 Cookies, p.165-167

CHEWY CHOCOLATE BROWNIES

Makes 12 brownies

These brownies deliver an intense chocolate experience with every bite.

1 cup all-purpose flour	*250 mL*
1 cup icing sugar	*250 mL*
4 1/2 tablespoons cocoa powder	*60 mL*
1 teaspoon baking powder	*5 mL*
1 1/2 ounces semisweet chocolate, coarsely chopped	*45 g*
3 tablespoons butter or margarine	*45 mL*
1/2 cup brown sugar	*125 mL*
2 tablespoons light corn syrup	*25 mL*
1/3 cup water	*75 mL*
2 teaspoons vanilla extract	*10 mL*
2 egg whites	*2*

Preheat oven to 350 F / 180 C.
Line an 8-inch/20cm square baking pan with aluminum foil. Coat foil with non-stick cooking spray. Set aside.
Sift flour, icing sugar, cocoa and baking powder onto a sheet of wax paper. In a medium saucepan over low heat, melt chocolate with butter. Remove from heat and stir in brown sugar, corn syrup, water and vanilla until well blended. Using a wooden spoon, beat egg whites into chocolate mixture. Gently stir in flour mixture until smooth and well blended. Transfer batter to prepared pan and smooth top with a spatula. Bake 24 to 28 minutes or until middle is firm when tapped. Let stand 15 minutes. Using any exposed foil as handles, carefully lift brownies out of pan and onto a wire rack. When completely cool, peel off foil and cut brownies into 12 squares.

nutrient analysis per serving	**Total Energy: 164 calories**
	Fat: 5 g
	Saturated Fat: 1 g
	Cholesterol: trace
	Sodium: 91 mg

CHOCOLATE CAKE WITH COCOA FROSTING

Serves 12

Be sure to use the best cocoa and chocolate you can find.

5 ounces semisweet chocolate	*150 g*
1/4 cup egg substitute	*50 mL*

1 egg, separated	*1*
1 teaspoon vanilla extract	*5 mL*
1 egg white	*1*
1/8 teaspoon cream of tartar	*0.5 mL*
1/2 cup cocoa powder	*125 mL*
2 tablespoons all-purpose flour	*25 mL*
2/3 cup plus 1/4 cup granulated sugar	*150 mL + 50 mL*
3/4 cup 1% milk	*175 mL*

Preheat oven to 350 F / 180 C.

Line bottom of an 8-inch/20cm round cake pan with parchment paper. Spray sides with non-stick cooking spray.

Place chocolate in a large mixing bowl. In a separate bowl, combine egg substitute, egg yolk and vanilla. Place 2 egg whites in a third bowl with the cream of tartar. Set aside.

Combine cocoa, flour and 2/3 cup/150 mL sugar in a large saucepan. Whisk in enough milk to make a smooth paste. Mix in remaining milk. Cook over medium heat until mixture begins to simmer. Cook gently, stirring constantly, 1 1/2 minutes. Pour hot mixture immediately over chopped chocolate and stir until chocolate is melted and smooth. Whisk in egg and vanilla mixture and set aside.

Beat egg whites at medium speed until soft peaks form. Gradually add remaining sugar, beating at high speed until stiff but not dry. Mix one-third of the egg whites into chocolate mixture to lighten it, then fold in remaining whites. Pour into prepared pan and smooth top with spatula.

Place cake pan in an ovenproof baking dish. Fill dish half-way with warm water and place in oven. Bake for exactly 30 minutes. The surface of the cake should spring back when gently pressed but will still be soft inside. Remove cake pan from water bath and let cool completely. Wrap in plastic and refrigerate overnight.

Run a thin knife around edge of pan to release the cake. Place a piece of parchment over top and flip onto a plate. Ice carefully with Cocoa Frosting.

Cocoa Frosting:

1 cup icing sugar	*250 mL*
2 tablespoons cocoa powder	*25 mL*
2 tablespoons light corn syrup	*25 mL*
2 tablespoons hot water	*25 mL*

Combine all ingredients and blend until smooth.

nutrient analysis per serving	**Total Energy: 239 calories** **Fat: 8 g** **Saturated Fat: 3 g** **Cholesterol: 19 mg** **Sodium: 43 mg**

MANGO SORBET WITH BLUEBERRY COMPOTE

Serves 10

Almost any soft fruit can be used in this sorbet. I used mango because the flavour and colour contrast beautifully with the blueberries.

5 ripe mangoes, peeled and seeded	*5*
1 1/2 teaspoons fresh lemon juice	*7 mL*
1/8 teaspoon salt	*0.5 mL*
1 cup Simple Syrup*	*250 mL*
3 cups blueberries	*750 mL*
1/2 cup granulated sugar	*125 mL*
1/2 cinnamon stick	*1/2*
1/2 cup apple cider or juice	*125 mL*

Place mango pulp in a food processor. Purée pulp, then strain through a medium sieve. You should have about 2 1/2 cups/625 mL. Transfer mango purée to a large bowl and add lemon juice, salt and Simple Syrup. Stir well and freeze according to ice cream machine instructions.

In a saucepan over medium heat, combine berries, sugar, cinnamon and cider. Slowly bring to a simmer, stirring occasionally to prevent sticking. Cook until liquid is slightly thickened and berries are fully cooked, 20 to 30 minutes. Remove from heat and let cool to room temperature. Remove cinnamon stick.

To serve, spoon compote into 10 dessert bowls. Scoop sorbet on top.

* Recipe page 138

nutrient analysis	Total Energy: 177 calories
	Fat: trace
	Saturated Fat: 0 g
per serving	Cholesterol: 0 mg
	Sodium: 35 mg

TOASTED ANGEL FOOD CAKE WITH PUMPKIN CHIFFON

Serves 12

As with any meringue-based recipe, it is important that there be no yolk or fat present when whipping egg whites. Even the smallest speck will prevent the whites from obtaining stiff peaks. Pumpkin chiffon adds a supple richness to this dessert.

Angel Food Cake:

1 1/2 cups granulated sugar	375 mL
1/2 cup cake and pastry flour	125 mL
1/4 teaspoon salt	1 mL
16 egg whites	16
2 teaspoons vanilla extract	10 mL
2 teaspoons cream of tartar	10 mL

Preheat oven to 350 F / 180 C.
In a dry bowl, combine 1/2 cup/125 mL sugar with flour and salt. In a separate bowl, whip egg whites until foamy. Add vanilla and cream of tartar. Beat to soft peaks. Gradually whip in remaining sugar and continue beating to stiff peaks. Sift dry ingredients over egg whites and fold together quickly but gently. Pour batter into an ungreased tube pan and smooth top with a spatula. Bake immediately until cake springs back when touched and cake tester comes out clean, 40 to 50 minutes. Remove cake from oven and immediately invert pan onto the neck of a bottle. Allow to cool upside down.

Pumpkin Chiffon:

1/2 cup granulated sugar	125 mL
1/2 cup boiling water	125 mL
1 tablespoon unflavoured gelatine	15 mL
1/4 cup water	50 mL
1/2 cup brown sugar, firmly packed	125 mL
1/4 cup egg substitute	50 mL
1/4 teaspoon ground ginger	1 mL
1/8 teaspoon nutmeg	0.5 mL
1/4 teaspoon cinnamon	1 mL
16-ounce can pumpkin	454 g
1 cup evaporated skim milk	250 mL
1/2 teaspoon salt	2mL
1/4 cup meringue powder*	50mL
1 tablespoon vanilla	15 mL

In a bowl, dissolve sugar in boiling water. Set aside.

Combine gelatine and water in a small bowl.

In a large saucepan, combine brown sugar, egg substitute, spices, pumpkin, evaporated milk and salt. Bring to a boil over medium heat, stirring constantly. Remove from heat and add gelatine mixture, stirring until dissolved. Pour into a dry bowl and refrigerate until slightly thickened. Add meringue powder to reserved sugar and water mixture. Beat until soft peaks form. Add vanilla and beat another minute. Fold meringue into pumpkin mixture until incorporated. Cover and refrigerate until needed.

Preheat oven broiler.

Slice angel food cake into 12 portions, place on cookie sheet and lightly broil until golden brown, 1 to 2 minutes. Turn slices over and repeat on other side. Remove from oven and transfer slices to individual dessert plates. Top each slice with pumpkin chiffon.

*Available at specialty food stores and bake shops.

nutrient analysis	Total Energy: 274 calories
	Fat: trace
	Saturated Fat: trace
per serving	Cholesterol: 1 mg
	Sodium: 265 mg

Glossary

BASMATI: A type of rice grown in the foothills of the Himalayas, known for its slim, slightly curved grains and aromatic, nutty flavour. This flavour is obtained by aging the grains for many years. True Basmati is unique in that it doubles in length instead of width as most rice grains do.

BISQUE: A classical soup made from the purée of crustaceans or vegetables. Usually thickened with rice and finished with heavy cream.

BLANCH: To cook briefly in boiling water to shorten final preparation time, remove strong odors, set the colour or to make skins easier to remove.

BOUQUET GARNI: A tied bundle of herbs, spices and aromatic vegetables such as leeks and celery.

CALORIE: The unit of measure for the energy value of foods. 1 calorie = 1 kilocalorie.

CHIFFON: A chiffon is similar to a thickened custard except that whipped egg whites are folded in.

CHIPOTLE: A dried, smoked mature jalapeno. Available dried or canned in adobo sauce, stewed with onions, tomatoes, vinegar and spices.

CHOLESTEROL: A waxy, fat-like substance made by the body and found in animal foods. Although cholesterol is essential for life, too much cholesterol in the blood increases the risk of heart disease. The highest concentration is in organ meat and egg yolks.

CORIANDER: The leafy green herb of the coriander plant is also known as cilantro or Asian parsley.

COMPOTE: Any fruit-based dish cooked in syrup and flavoured with spices and/or liqueurs.

COULIS: Any purée of vegetables or fruit that is passed through a sieve to remove solid pieces of skin or seed.

COURT-BOUILLON: "Short broth" in French. This savoury liquid, similar to a stock, is used to steam and poach many food items, especially fish. Court-bouillon is usually vegetable-based and includes fresh herbs, carrots, leeks, celery, wine or vinegar.

DEGLAZE: To dissolve and release the reduced drippings in a sauté or roasting pan with the addition of a liquid such as wine or stock.

DREDGE: To coat food with any dry ingredient such as cornmeal, flour or breadcrumbs.

EGG SUBSTITUTE: Components of egg substitute vary by manufacturer. Most contain egg whites with added natural colours and stabilizers to give them the colour and texture of beaten whole eggs. One-quarter cup (50 mL) of substitute is equal to one egg.

FRICASSEE: A stew of white meat or poultry, traditionally served with a white sauce.

GRANITA: A coarse frozen dessert of French and Italian origin. A fine version of granita is called sorbet. Granita contains no fat or cholesterol.

GUMBO FILÉ: The powdered dry leaves and bark of the sassafras tree, native to the southern United States and Central America. Also called filé powder.

JULIENNE: A thin, stick-shaped vegetable cut, usually 1/8-inch/0.2 cm square and 2 inches/5 cm long.

MEDALLION: A cut of meat, usually from the loin, that is round in shape and equal in thickness.

MIREPOIX: A basic flavouring agent of aromatic vegetables. Usually includes carrots, celery, leeks or onions, herbs and peppercorns.

MISO: A fermented, aged soybean paste used extensively in Japanese cuisine.

OKRA: Okra is a relative of the hibiscus. Its unripened pods are used as a vegetable and as a thickening agent. Originally from tropical Africa, it was brought to North America with the slave trade in the 18th century. Okra is now widely cultivated in the southern United States.

OMEGA-3 FATTY ACIDS: A polyunsaturated fat commonly found in fish and fish oils as well as in canola oil, soybeans and flaxseed. They play a role in reducing the risk of heart disease and are also required for normal growth and development and for good vision.

PARCHMENT: A heat-resistant paper used for lining pans and trays and covering items to be shallow-poached.

PAD THAI: A fried noodle dish native to Thailand. Usually served as a lunch or midday snack with other side dishes.

POACH: To gently cook in lightly simmering liquid.

PUREE: To chop until extremely fine or smooth.

RAFT: The coagulation of egg whites and other proteins to form a solid mass in a consommé as it clarifies the liquid.

REDUCE: To boil a liquid until original volume has decreased; to concentrate existing flavour, colour and body of a liquid.

ROUX: A combination of fat and flour in a certain proportion used to thicken soups and sauces.

SATURATED FAT: A hard, solid fat at room temperature. Saturated fats raise the level of cholesterol and triglycerides in the blood. Sources include butter, lard, meat, poultry, milk products (except skim milk), palm and coconut oils.

SAUTE: To cook quickly in small amounts in a sauté pan. The pan should be hot enough to make the items "jump" in the pan. Sauté means " jumped" in French.

SHOCK: To chill immediately, usually in ice water, to stop the cooking process.

STEEP: To soak highly flavoured or coloured items in warm liquid to extract these properties.

SUPREME: The breast portion of any bird, deboned except for part of the wing bone.

SWEAT: To cook over low heat until items (usually aromatic vegetables) release their liquid or juices.

TAMARI: A dark, intensely-flavoured soy sauce brewed without the addition of wheat or rice.

TANDOORI PASTE: An Indian spice paste made bright red by the annatto seed.

TOGARASHI PEPPER: A Japanese seasoning containing chili flakes, beefsteak tomato seed, dried orange peel and seaweed.

TORTILLA: An unleavened corn or flour flatbread native to the southern United States and Central America.

TRIGLYCERIDES: A type of fat found in the blood. Like cholesterol, it is affected by your food choices, mainly excessive fat, alcohol and sugar.

UNSATURATED FAT: Usually a liquid at room temperature. This type of fat helps to lower the level of cholesterol and triglycerides in the blood when substituted for saturated fat. It is found mainly in plant foods. There are two main types:
1. Monounsaturates – sources include canola, peanut and olive oil and their margarines.
2. Polyunsaturates – sources include safflower, sunflower, corn and soybean oils and their margarines.

VINAIGRETTE: An emulsion of oil and vinegar in a certain proportion, used as a cold sauce for items such as salad.

VINE RIPENED: Any fruit or vegetable that has reached full maturity and ripeness while still attached to its vine.

Index